WOMEN ARTISANS OF
MOROCCO

THEIR STORIES, THEIR LIVES

SUSAN SCHAEFER DAVIS

PHOTOGRAPHY BY JOE COCA

Editor: Carol Karasik
Publisher: Linda Ligon
Associate Publisher: Karen Brock
Design: Michael Angelo Signorella

Cover image: Aicha Seqqat, president of the Timnay Association
of weavers in N'kob, Morocco

THRUMS
BOOKS
306 North Washington Avenue
Loveland, Colorado 80537
USA

Printed in China by Asia Pacific
Library of Congress Control Number: 2017954858

ACKNOWLEDGEMENTS

My parents got me started on the path that led to this book, my father by teaching me to be curious and my mother by showing me how to see and appreciate beauty.

I thank them, and all the others who have contributed.

The Peace Corps sent me to Morocco to work in a rural women's center in 1965, and that connection with Morocco and her women was a real gift, one that's lasted all my life. Moroccan women, especially the rural ones, have motivated me to work with them as an academic, a development consultant, and a project founder, selling their rugs. One of the first was Aicha Qasm, who came to the women's center. Their wisdom, strength, warmth, humor, and skills continually inspire me. The women who shared their stories made this book possible.

Other women who have inspired me are the members of Weave A Real Peace (WARP) http://weavearealpeace.org, a group whose mission is to foster a global network of enthusiasts who value the importance of textiles to grassroots economies. Their annual meetings, usually in the U.S., provide face-to-face contact with about thirty to fifty women with an interest in worldwide textiles as well as talks and workshops on a local textile tradition. I always leave feeling invigorated. Deborah Chandler was the founder, and she and the late Alice Brown are two of these inspiring women.

Another inspirational member of WARP is Linda Ligon, publisher of this series of books. Her enthusiasm and dedication are making possible an archive of information on weavers' lives and textile work in many cultures, and I thank her for inviting me to participate. Photographer Joe Coca was a joy to work with, enjoying Moroccan culture—and cuisine—and charming the artisans and their children. Naoual Ouakrim translated when I interviewed the southern Tashelhit (Berber-speaking) women, allowing me to communicate with them in depth for the first time, although I had known them for years. Later in the process, my editor Carol Karasik really helped me to enliven the text, and Linda's associate publisher Karen Brock was very helpful and supportive as the project drew near a close.

Dan Driscoll, the founder of the national cooperative Anou, and his team of artisans are implementing a model that empowers Moroccan artisans to sell their products using smartphones, even if they are illiterate. Anou allows the artisan, not a middleman, to profit from her work. This enlarges the vision I had when I began MarrakeshExpress.org, and I am very grateful that this work is being carried on.

My husband Douglas and daughter Laila have always supported my work in Morocco, living there for long stretches, learning Arabic, and loving the people; it's been wonderful to have them involved. My Moroccan daughter Halima Benayad was born there but now lives in the United States and was especially helpful in understanding many of the interviews, including the meanings and subtle senses of certain words. Her friend Khadija Izghi was very helpful with rug terms.

I feel very lucky to have had the support of all these people, who have helped make this book possible.

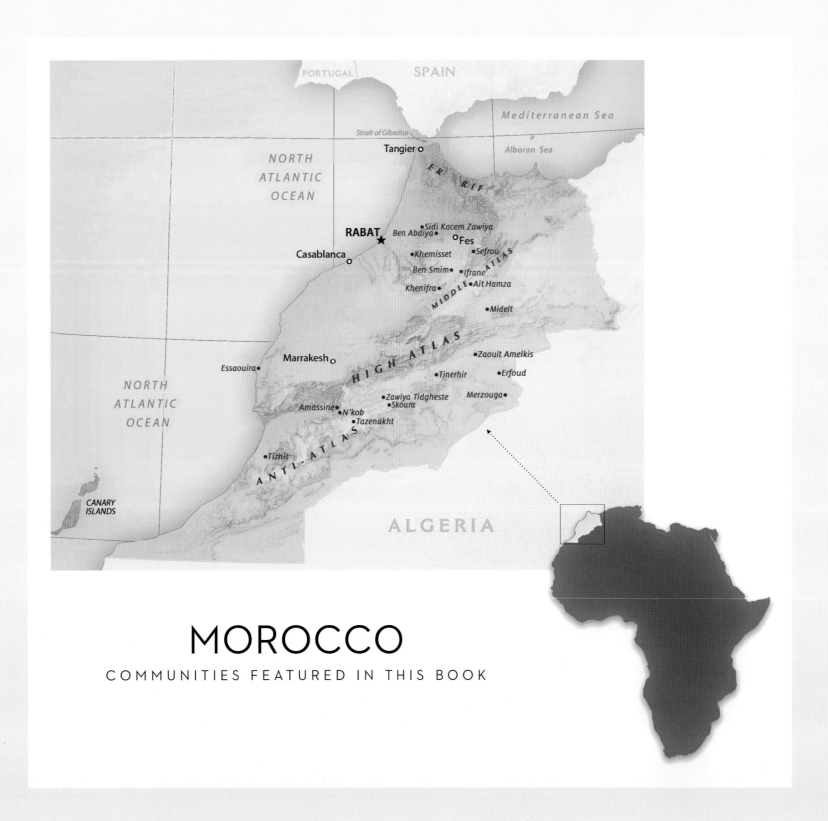

MOROCCO

COMMUNITIES FEATURED IN THIS BOOK

CONTENTS

INTRODUCTION

MOROCCO IS A FEAST FOR THE SENSES. Ancient cities and villages resound with the music of *oud* and flute, exotic aromas waft from secret doorways as women draped in dusty rose and sky blue go about their daily chores, sometimes wearing under these robes spangled gowns for weekend festivals. Even the horses are decorated in lavish trappings for festivals. Pattern is everywhere, in the neatly stacked vegetables in street stalls and inside houses, embellishing pottery, tile mosaics, brass work, and carved wood. Geometric rug designs are underfoot, softening the tile floor, warming families in winter. Stars are stitched into embroidered clothes and buttons. Much of this intricate geometry is created by women.

For a taste of their varied artistry, wander through the *souks*, the weekly open-air markets where weavers often sell their latest work. Of course, most people are there to purchase basic household needs. Rural families grow their own wheat or olives but depend on the markets that circulate from town to town for mint, chickpeas, dates, and fresh meat and vegetables. Aside from tasty foodstuffs, the traveling merchants often haul in manufactured goods to sell from their makeshift stalls; among the charcoal braziers and spices are stacks of imported kitchen gadgets, used clothing, or tools. Meanwhile a vendor with a microphone is extolling his cure for bedbugs, barbers are cutting men's hair, tailors are stitching dresses on their treadle sewing machines, dentists are pulling teeth, and herbalists are treating the sick. Just past the spot where the water seller is filling a customer's brass cup stand the stalls where weavers are buying supplies: raw and spun wool, white or dyed; synthetic warp threads; twisted yarn from unraveled sweaters, used for making "rag" rugs. The next stall is the place to purchase hand cards, combs, beaters to pound the wool weft, and special scissors to trim rug surfaces.

Off in one corner are the rug sellers. The Tuesday souk in the large town of Khemisset offers a permanent covered area where merchants put their rugs on display. The older men in their brown *jellabas* (outer garments) and the younger ones sporting jeans and leather jackets are no match for the brilliant wares they are hawking, and the weavers who go from one to the other trying to sell their work are no match for the men. Although Aicha Duha and a few of her friends have permanent stalls, female rug merchants are a rare sight in Morocco. In the southern rug area of Tazenakht, women seldom attend the main Thursday market. Yet growing numbers of weavers are participating in the "women's rug market" held the night before. This relatively new development is a major step toward encouraging more women to sell their work directly. However, they must be canny, because the buyers are mostly middlemen who offer low prices.

One thing that hasn't changed is that people have come to buy, bargain, and have fun. They have traveled by donkey, horse-drawn carts, graceful carriages, and motorbikes. Souk day is a time for meeting friends, enjoying a treat of barbecued beef or nougat candy, or attracting a future spouse. Myriad sights, sounds, and smells drift from the stalls.

This book is about women's devotion to their craft. While there are numerous volumes about Moroccan rugs, embroidery, and costume, none focus on the artisans who produce these beautiful pieces while maintaining households and raising children. Textile

Souk merchant in Marrakesh.

fabrics and luxury brocades have traditionally been the province of men. At a time when female artisans are becoming middlewomen and are beginning to take control of their products, this book explores their work and their lives and how the two are interrelated and evolving, often to empower them.

Most of the women presented here are rug weavers whose ancient skills and designs vary from region to region. Fes embroidery, similar to cross-stitch, is also an esteemed female craft. Fine embroidered bed and table linens, once essential in bridal trousseaus, remain highly coveted in many modern households. Another basic, needle-woven buttons, have decorated native costumes for centuries, but the styles have grown more elaborate in women's hands. The same is true for custom-made apparel. Seamstresses, who have long been engaged in sewing women's everyday garments, are slowly replacing tailors and creating both jellabas and the elaborate gowns worn for celebrations.

This creative burst is taking place in a Muslim country of thirty-four million people who dwell in busy cities and isolated villages dotting a dramatic and varied landscape. Morocco is much like California in geography and climate. Coastal beaches on the Atlantic and Mediterranean offer resorts and fishing. Fertile plains produce wheat, olives, and citrus. Wild mountain ranges are snowcapped in winter and provide grazing, terraced irrigated fields near villages, and sometimes saffron in spring. Beyond the forested mountains stretches the endless desert interrupted by scattered oases.

Much of Morocco's population, and most of the traditional artisans in this book, are Berber, or as they prefer to be called, Amazigh, meaning "free people." Indeed, a fierce independent streak marks the history of this once-powerful civilization. During Biblical times, Berber tribes vied with Carthage and Egypt for commercial dominance in the region. Seven hundred years later, the "Moors" invaded Spain, introducing advanced science and mathematics to the European continent mired in the Dark Ages. The Moroccan kingdom's advantageous position as a major crossroads between Europe, the Middle East, and sub-Saharan Africa also meant that the Berbers played reluctant hosts to many foreign cultures. Phoenicians, Romans, Spanish, and Portuguese succes-

Overlooking the great city of Fes.

Left: Rug merchants in Marrakesh.
Right: Intricate tile, carved wood, and carved and painted plaster mosaic work in Fes.

sively controlled the lucrative trade routes, only to leave behind monumental ruins. The influence of these cultures on women's textiles is obscured by time, though one woman told me that the Roman mosaics at Volubilis were rugs that had turned to stone.

Roman walls were crumbling when Arabs migrated from the east, bringing the riches of Classical learning with them. Morocco adopted Islam and took on an Arabic name, Al Maghrib al Aqsa, which means "the furthest west" of the Muslim countries. In AD 789, King Idris I founded Fes, today the world's largest functioning *medina* and a major center for Moroccan artisans. Despite the adoption of Arabic customs, language, and religion, the Berbers never relinquished their identity and periodically swept down from their mountain strongholds. Centuries of uprisings eventually led to an uneasy truce. But that tentative reconciliation could not withstand the French invasion of 1912. After forty-four years of colonization, the country finally achieved independence in 1956. The Kingdom of Morocco is now a constitutional monarchy governed by the heir of the ancient Alaouite royal dynasty as well as by an elected parliament. The current ruler, Mohammed VI, is often called "the poor people's king" because he has established dozens of programs aimed at improving socioeconomic conditions. These include training centers for women artisans. The centers (*nadis*) teach sewing, embroidery, knitting, and crochet, the same crafts that well-bred young ladies in the major cities learned from skilled craftswomen in earlier times, and that I taught when I was in the Peace Corps. Nadis remain popular, and although

one may wonder if the young women are initially attracted by the crafts or the social contact, many have gone on to become expert artisans who have worked themselves free of poverty.

Strength and Spirit—Women in Transition

Morocco is developing rapidly. When I first arrived in the 1960s, the majority of the population lived in rural areas whereas today 60 percent of the population is urban. Fifty years ago there were few good roads, but now cars and trucks crisscross the country on paved highways and divided freeways. People who once depended on souks or small stores for their basic needs now shop at supermarkets and large malls. There was one telephone in the village of 5,000 where I lived during my Peace Corps days. Today,

Horse competition near Sidi Kacem Zawiya.

Above: Fadma Buhassi tends the bread oven in her courtyard.
Top Right: Ijja Id Ali Boufkir prepares a meal at her home in N'kob.
Bottom Right: an artisan paints ceramic cups at a pottery workshop in Fes.

nearly everyone has a cell phone and access to the Internet. With the rise in the standard of living, more women work outside the home, and the average number of children per family has dropped from 7.2 to 2.2.

Education has had a profound effect on the lives of artisans. Under the French, public schooling was almost nonexistent, but since the 1950s, the Moroccan government has slowly improved educational opportunities in rural areas. It is not surprising, then, that most elder women have never attended school, while those under forty years of age usually have a primary or high school education. Three women in this book hold university degrees, and although they love their craft and do all they can to assist artisans, they rely on other sources for earning a living. There's no telling what may happen to these honorable skills in the future.

The weavers, button makers, and embroiderers who appear in these pages were mainly chosen for their outstanding abilities. The ages, education levels, and urban or rural residence vary among the artisans, so this is a sampling from many groups. Because most of these women live in rural villages, they provide an intimate view of traditional life in a country where customs and social roles are in flux. The nine women who live in cities or remain single present a unique portrait of a society in transition. The three artisans who have become middlewomen, activists, and entrepreneurs reveal the amazing possibilities open to women in Morocco today.

Moroccan artisans lead a hard life. In addition to practicing their craft, they cook three meals a day, feed the cows and sheep in rural areas, wash clothes by hand, and some haul water from the village well. But these Moroccan women do enjoy certain freedoms. Unlike women in Saudi Arabia and in areas dominated by the Taliban, they can drive, attend school, and work outside the home. In fact, these drastic prohibitions are the exceptions rather than the rule throughout the Arab world. Egypt's feminist movement began in the early 1920s, and almost a century later, young women played a vital role during Egypt's "Arab Spring." When I visited Iraq in 1999, I met with the Minister of Information, a woman in her fifties who was no stranger to government power. From my first contact with Moroccan women in the 1960s, I was struck by their openness, intelligence, and wit. They did not sit quietly and wait to be given orders or

lessons. They laughed, told ribald jokes, and sometimes got into hair-pulling fights.

Despite the reality, the Western stereotype of male-dominated, submissive Muslim women persists. The fact is that up until the 1970s, most information on Muslim women came from male observers. In the presence of men, especially foreign men, women, if seen at all, are expected to enter a room serving food, silently with eyes downcast. This is how they are taught to behave and certainly gives the impression of submission. When female scholars, both Western and Middle Eastern, started studying the everyday lives of Muslim women, they were able to interact with women in their own domain, as men could not, and so their reports presented a much fuller picture. Yet the stereotypes endured.

With increased interest in the Middle East during the first Iraq War, I was expecting that views on Muslim women would go beyond the stereotypes. Instead, the media focused on Saudi Arabia, which practices one of the most conservative versions of Islam. Why did the media emphasize the most egregious examples of Islam? It's been suggested that this strategy—to "save" women—was designed to increase Western support for military operations in the Middle East and Afghanistan.

Women in Morocco do not live under similar bans and when left to themselves are far from submissive. Universally, single-sex groups are empowering. In women's colleges in the United States, women fill all the leadership roles. In women's associations in Morocco, talents also come to the fore. There is the best organizer, the best informed about the neighborhood, the one who travels and knows her way around the capital, or the one who can sell embroidery or rugs through her connections.

How do Moroccan women react to male dominance? All too often I've heard men say, "Women are worthless." Moroccan women are always quick to react, often saying, "Men are worthless." One woman told her son-in-law, "You're like that watch you wear: it gives the time, but it's never right."

Years ago, the same woman's father had promised her to an older man she didn't like. When he brought her family a wedding gift of grapes, henna, and a few chickens, she dumped them on the ground. The chickens pecked at the grapes and mixed them with the henna, ruining the lot. Her angry father shackled her ankles as

Fadma Buhassi's daughter in a style of veiling not used in Morocco today.

family is still headed by a strong, macho father, but Mama runs the household behind the scenes. This is similar to Southern U.S. women, who are often described as the iron fist in the velvet glove. Moroccan women have independent ideas, and like many women, rely on skillful management rather than confrontation.

If given an inch, Moroccan women will take a mile. Increasingly, women are assuming an active role in fighting abuses. In the face of domestic violence, many women's groups are working to change the laws. In 2004, Morocco was the regional poster child for the reform of laws related to family, such as raising the age of marriage and granting women greater rights in divorce and child custody cases. Although these laws are not yet fully implemented, women are taking matters into their own hands and groups are working for change.

The struggle for equality is taking place on many levels. In 2012, fifty-six years after independence, 17 percent of the Moroccan parliament was composed of female members, almost as many as in the U.S. Congress after more than 200 years. A few years earlier, Amina Yabis, the button maker (page 118), ran for local office, just to show that it could be done. Aicha Duha (page 34) supports a family of four by serving as a middlewoman in a male domain. As a little girl, Fadma Wadal (page 14) stole wool off the sheep she was herding and hid it under a gravestone at night, because she was so eager to learn to spin and weave. These actions belie the stereotype of passive, submissive Muslim women.

Wearing the Veil

Many of the same women who are fighting for equal rights choose to wear the veil, an article of clothing that is widely interpreted as a symbol of oppression. For many Westerners, why, and how, Muslim women wear the veil is a mystery. The custom has its roots in ancient religious teachings that regard women as objects of temptation. Yet the Quran does not clearly state that women should veil. The closest statement is in *surah* 24:30–31:

> And say to the believing women that they should lower their gaze and guard their modesty; that they should not display their beauty and ornaments except what must ordinarily appear thereof; that they should draw their veil over their breasts and not display their beauty except to their husband, their fathers . . . [and other male relatives].

punishment. Instead of submitting, she and a girlfriend worked off one shackle, which she slung over her shoulder, and ran off to the farm of a French colonist. When her father came looking for her, the Frenchman told him that if he forced his daughter to marry, he'd report him to the authorities. The young woman ended up marrying a man of her choosing.

That incident happened in the 1940s, so assertive women are not new; they were just not recognized. The typical Moroccan

As in many religious traditions, much is open to interpretation. The Hadith, or sayings of the Prophet, is less ambiguous on the subject. In deference to tradition and ideals of modesty, women who wear the veil do so in the presence of nonfamily members. At home or in a group of women, they lay it aside. At the women's center where I taught, women removed their veils when they sewed.

Customs and styles vary from country to country. The word *hijab,* often used to refer to veiling today, literally means a curtain or screen in Arabic, and it generally refers to a shawl covering the head or a larger fabric swathing the whole body except for the face, hands, and feet. In Afghanistan, women wear the *burqa,* a full-body covering with a fabric "screen" that allows them to see through, whereas the *niqab* worn in Yemen has a narrow slit for the eyes. The *abaya* of Iran is a long black cloth draped over the head and body but not the face. Moroccan veiling is a more liberal version that has varied over time. The few who have recently adopted the more conservative styles are apparently inspired by stricter interpretations of Islam.

Veiling has changed so drastically over the past fifty years that I'd have to say it is subject to both political shifts and fashion trends. When I first arrived in 1965, the outer robe (jellaba) had a large hood that covered the hair and forehead like a nun's wimple. In addition, women wore a veil that covered the face below the eyes. The effect was not the same as the slitted niqab. Women could see well through the generous space, and with good eye makeup and a gauzy veil (after all, it was the sixties), the effect was very attractive. Virtually all married women in cities and towns dressed this way. In rural areas, where women worked in the fields, it was less common to cover the face. They did cover their hair with wrapped and tied headscarves.

Nearly twenty years before I arrived, King Mohammed's aunt took off her veil while delivering a nationalist speech about women's important contribution to the country. Yet most women did not follow her example. However, from 1965 until the early 1980s, there was a gradual moving away from a veil covering the face, and sometimes the hair as well.

Beginning in 1982, there was another dramatic shift when the movement toward Arabization, especially in education and gov-

A traditional jellaba and veil as worn in the 1960s.

ernment, led to a general rejection of the colonial language and, indeed, all things French. People began decorating their salons with mosaic tiles and replacing their French couches and gauzy drapes with richly upholstered brocaded banquettes. This sense of pride in their Arabic heritage, something the French had deprecated, extended to clothing. Women began to wear jellabas and other long garments more often. It was rumored that Islamist groups were distributing these other garments to college students. If true, this act of propaganda certainly saved money and made everyday

Aicha Duha (page 34) enjoys a visit with Susan Schaefer Davis.

life more convenient. Unfortunately, the long gray coats with huge buttons down the front were ugly. In time, the traditional jellaba went from a dark, boxy garment of stiff polyester fabric to a slender version in softer cloth and a gorgeous array of colors.

And women began covering their hair again. Instead of scarves, they started wearing head coverings that hugged the face. They also turned from dull, dark colors to bright hues coordinated with their jellabas. Sometimes they decorated the fabric with appliqués or rhinestones.

A completely different style of hijab entered Morocco from the far south. Women there wear the *milhaf*, a long cloth that covers the head and body. Unlike the black abaya worn in Iran and Saudi Arabia, the milhaf is made of colorful tie-dyed fabric that women wrap around themselves instead of holding it in place with their hands.

After several years of tightly bound head coverings, urban women took to wearing looser scarves, which left a few strands of hair peeking out. Some women, especially university students, uncovered their hair completely, though they still dressed in modest long-sleeved tops over long skirts or trousers. Others continued to cover their heads but adopted tight sweaters and jeans. The incredible variety suggests that hijab is as much a fashion statement as a religious one. When best friends walk hand in hand down the street, one in hijab, the other not, they seem to be saying that no one can tell them what to do in a country that is becoming an open society.

In fact, Islam states that wearing hijab should be a woman's own choice, not to be made lightly. Older and rural women do it more out of habit than religious motivation. It is how they have always dressed, and they would be embarrassed to uncover their heads. More educated and younger urban women are more likely to do it for religious reasons, or for style.

Far from being an instrument of oppression, the hijab has many meanings for the women who choose to wear it. A recent article published in *The Huffington Post* presented the views of young professional Muslim women living in the United States. For one woman, hijab reflects "beauty, sincerity, struggle, identity, strength, challenge, meaning, purpose, and most importantly my choice!" Another woman stated: "Hijab as a verb is the action of modesty in all aspects of my being . . . It is viewed as oppressive, but there is nothing more liberating than hijab. It is a signature of self-respect. It speaks to the people around me that you have no choice but to learn to *appreciate who* I am as a person, to learn my characteristics, morals, and values." Still another woman wrote, "The hijab is a constant reminder to stay cool and collected and do things that will please God. My hijab and my smile are an open invitation to Islam. An invitation to look past what you think you know of my religion and to see the true purpose of it, which is to be a good person and to spread peace in the world."

My Story

Everywhere in the world clothes are a necessity and a means of personal or cultural expression. How, then, did I get involved with Moroccan textiles?

I always liked sewing. I remember making doll clothes out of the four-inch squares of fabric from my grandfather's sample book for general stores in southern Minnesota. I made most of my clothes in high school. But now that I think of it, maybe it was really the textiles that I liked. I loved going to fabric stores, seeing all the colors and textures available when I was choosing material for a new dress.

That interest eventually led to my assignment as a Peace Corps volunteer in Morocco, teaching rural women how to knit and to sew on machines. (There wasn't much weaving in my area.) Morocco changed my life. I fell in love with the country and the people, especially the warmth and connection of a vibrant women's society. The experience turned me into an anthropologist. I wanted to understand why the women were so fun and feisty, not the passive, submissive beings I had read about in the pages of *National Geographic*. I went back to the United States and eventually explored that contradiction for my doctoral dissertation, which was later published as *Patience and Power*. I have been making the case for women's strength and agency since the 1970s and hope this book will contribute to that effort.

I taught at the university level for ten years, but found I preferred being in the field with Moroccan women rather than in a classroom with undergraduates. So I became a consultant on economic development for the World Bank, the Peace Corps, and USAID. My work focused on potable water projects, education programs for girls, microcredit for women, and child labor and youth activism issues in Morocco, Egypt, Jordan, Palestine, and Israel. Through those projects I was able to observe girls and women in different cultural contexts.

Before I left teaching, I began collecting Moroccan rugs. Friends in the States admired them, and soon I was buying and selling rugs to people back home. My husband was an early computer geek, and when I had the idea of selling online, he helped me set up a website, and in 1994 I became one of the first cyber-merchants.

After Marrakesh Express (www.marrakeshexpress.org) proved a success, I moved on to the next step: selling rugs directly, and pro bono, from weavers in two villages, N'kob and Ben Smim. By selling online the women could bypass the middlemen in the market and receive higher prices for their work, and reach a worldwide audience. The site shows photos of the rugs, along with a photo and brief biography of each weaver. In a way, I was still teaching about Moroccan culture, this time online to clients.

I worked with these women until 2016, when I encouraged them to join a new online group. Anou ("The Well"; www.theanou.com) takes my idea of online marketing to more expansive levels. Since marketing is so important for artisans, a full description of this innovative enterprise appears in the concluding chapter of this book.

Even though I have handed over Marrakesh Express, I am still teaching about Morocco by leading cultural and textile tours. My husband says they should be called "American friends of Susan meet Moroccan friends of Susan," because that's what we do. In addition to touring the major sites, we encourage social interchanges by visiting artisans and activists in their homes.

I was thrilled to be asked to write this book because it gave me an opportunity to increase my knowledge about crafts and their roles in women's lives. Some of the artisans are good friends, some are members of my "Moroccan family" dating back to Peace Corps days when their grandparents befriended me, and some are dynamic women whom I greatly admire. It was a joy to travel with Joe Coca, whose curiosity, sensibility, and fortitude never waivered as we moved through a strange land. His photographs capture the beauty of the women, their work, and Morocco. In photos and in interviews—even when I had to rely on a translator when speaking to Berber artisans—the women's personalities shine through.

Their Stories

Images of Morocco have been shaped by the media and by a generation of American writers like Paul Bowles and Tennessee

The dramatic landscape near Amassine in the Anti-Atlas Mountains south of Marrakesh.

Williams, who were drawn to the exotic yet kept their distance from the culture. By contrast, this book presents a close-up of its people. Storytellers like Fadma Wadal and her granddaughter Aziza (page 14) provide an intimate view of desert life as it was sixty years ago. Over the mountains in Marrakesh, Samira Benayad (page 110), a traditional seamstress, offers a glimpse of a married woman's life in the modern world.

Along the way the women explain the technical aspects of their crafts, the meaning of the designs, and their attitudes toward their work. Fatima Fdil of Ben Smim (page 22), who has been weaving for more than fifty years, tells us that a rug on the loom has a soul, and when it is cut off, the soul dies and is reborn into a new life in someone's home. For Jamila Samaa of N'kob (page 70), weaving is a creative act, and she sees her rugs as art. Most weavers in N'kob are more pragmatic and regard rug sales as an important way to help or even support their families with household expenses. Women like Fatima El Mennouny (page 66) have earned enough to help build a new home.

These artisans are models of strength, and their power is increased when they work in groups. The Assabirate Cooperative (page 145) is composed of women with disabilities whose superb embroidery affords greater self-reliance. Amina Yabis (page 118) is a tireless grassroots feminist who organizes button makers into self-sufficient cooperatives. After Kheira Ilahiane (page 96) organized a weaving association, she became involved in local politics as another way to help women achieve economic and social status. "Thank God that the king gave us our rights. And praise God that we're going to go further."

The delicate designs hidden in rugs, embroidery, and buttons represent flowers, insects, foodstuffs, tools, and more. It's almost impossible for the average eye to recognize these objects, much less learn their deeper meanings. As Kenza Oulaghda (page 86) tells us, handsaws and horse bridles symbolize the complementary relationship between men and women. In the changing society of modern-day Morocco, the overall pattern stands for pride and independence.

A DESERT LIFE

FADMA WADAL IS A FEISTY old woman—my favorite kind—and a great storyteller. She has seen a lot in her seventy years, from growing up in the remote village of Zawiya Tidgheste, south of the High Atlas Mountains, to traveling the country with her husband during his military service. She's herded camels and watched her grandchildren use smartphones. And she has plenty to say about the life of a woman and weaver surviving at the edge of the desert.

She regales her listeners in fluent Arabic, which is unusual for an elder Berber woman, but when I needed help with subtle details, her granddaughter Aziza gladly served as translator. When she did, she and Fadma would inevitably spin some lively family tale. It was obvious they had spent many evenings together, drinking mint tea and talking about Fadma's early life, because the young Aziza knew those stories by heart. Elsewhere in the world, television has eroded oral traditions, but in this rural family, the past is ever present.

The future is literally next door. Just over the hill lies Morocco's huge new solar energy project, Nur, whose giant mirrors radiating across the desert floor bring electricity to a million distant homes. But advanced technology is still out of reach here, apparently stalled by the old adobe ruins that surround the village. These abandoned multifamily living compounds were fortified, accessible by a single door, vital in times of political unrest when villages were threatened by raiding parties.

The area was once controlled by Thami El Glaoui, Lord of the Atlas, who collaborated with the French colonial powers before Moroccan independence in 1956. His troops occupied the village and mercilessly plundered crops and livestock. Anyone who rebelled risked being pounded into one of those thick adobe walls.

Today most people, including Fadma, live in concrete block houses. But the *qsar* where she was born is still standing, and an enterprising grandson has turned some rooms into a museum displaying old artifacts as well as an art gallery exhibiting his paintings. In the last few years the village population has dwindled to a few hundred souls, largely because of drought and a lack of jobs.

Fadma spent her childhood there and married when she was twelve. She hadn't reached puberty yet, and four years passed before she had children, four daughters and two sons in all. Three of her daughters moved to cities, leaving one daughter and the younger son in the village, where he grows wheat, barley, alfalfa, and some vegetables. The older son, now fifty-four, lives and works in France.

Fadma is proud of the way she raised her children. "My daughters and sons never got into arguments or fights with people. It was forbidden. If they said this one did this to me, that one did that, I'd say, 'Be quiet!' Now everyone tells me how well behaved they are. They don't cause a ruckus, they don't envy others their good fortune. I hope God may protect them, and I hope God provides for

Left: Adobe ruins at Zawiya Tidgheste.
Right: Fadma Wadal with one of her favorite covers that she wove.

A qsar near the village of Zawiya Tidgheste, where Fadma was born.

them so I can live with them and that they'll do good things for me, to repay me for all I've been through."

When Fadma was young, her father took a second wife. Instead of accepting the arrangement, her mother left and moved north to live with a sister's daughter. Social mores decreed that the child stay with the father, and so Fadma was abandoned and her mother lost her daughter. "She was really hurt, poor thing, and she had to leave me behind. My father took me away from my mother. I didn't even know where to sleep. I had a really hard time. Fortunately, my uncle's wife took me in. She carried me on her back, I slept with her, and she gave me food and drink."

Aziza broke in with a story from Fadma's childhood. "When she was about ten, she had some sickness. She had to sleep outside in a little corner, and one man stayed with her and took care of her. Until the sickness passed, no one could go near her. That sickness, it's not around here much since they do vaccinations. You get a fever and sleep a lot and can't talk at all. It may have been smallpox. My grandmother just wanted to die or for God to save her."

Fadma continued. "When I got a little bigger and the goats and sheep had babies, my aunt would say, 'Get up and take the animals out to the fields.' The sun would be warm, and I'd take them out and watch them. A few years later, we had camels. My aunt told me, 'Take sacks with you and gather grass and bring it back.' Until late afternoon I'd fill the bags and put them on the camels and bring them home. I'd even ride on the camels and go loping along, bumpety, bumpety, bump."

"Wait, let me tell her!" Aziza interrupted. "She got on a camel and it started to run. She held onto it and grabbed it with her feet down by its belly. That tickled it, and it got scared and ran. It ran away and she was on it. She was screaming and holding on to the camel as tight as she could. It ran and ran a long ways, maybe a kilometer."

Fadma chimed in. "That camel ran away with me. I screamed, the women who were with me screamed, 'Fadma died, Fadma died!' Then the camel stopped. She folded her legs and sat down. I shouted and shouted, but she wouldn't get up. She sat there until the other camels caught up. The women came and said, 'Thank goodness you're okay!' My father came too, and I said, 'That's it, Papa! You abandoned me. You didn't even try to run and catch me!' He said, 'I was praying for you, daughter.'" With that, Fadma and Aziza burst into laughter.

When Fadma was still a shepherdess, she learned to card, spin, and weave. She used a raw fig as the whorl of her spindle. She made her little loom out of sticks and wove some small samplers while she was out tending the sheep. She'd pull some wool off a ewe's stomach, where it wouldn't show, and on her way home she'd hide the wool under a gravestone in the cemetery. The next day, she'd retrieve the wool and take it along to the fields. "If people saw me spinning, they'd ask me, 'Where did you find that wool?' I'd say, a Jewish lady gave it to me. There were Jewish families in our village. They were really good. They helped people. After a while I spun like an expert, and I was really fast too.

"Sometimes I'd ask a woman to teach me. I'd go to her home and I'd say, 'Please, can I be with you an hour or so, just to learn a little? If you teach me, God will reward you.' I'd go in and start weaving with the woman, and she'd say, 'Why, my girl, you've already learned!' And I'd say, 'It's these eyes that learn.'"

"And your brain," Aziza added.

"It's the eyes and the desire that teach people," Fadma said. "Without them I wouldn't know anything. The lady said, 'It's like you're on fire. You learned well!'"

That was before she was married off at twelve.

"After I got married, my husband's relatives wanted me to cook the meals, get grass and alfalfa for the animals, and go down to the river to collect firewood. I'd do everything. At night I'd weave. People in our village loved weaving, and I wanted to be like the others."

As an old woman, Fadma doesn't weave any more. But in the past she made pile rugs, men's capes and robes, bridal capes, and floor coverings. In the old days, the men's capes were woven with a rounded bottom edge, but that skill has almost disappeared. Today the capes are finished with square edges and rounded by a tailor.

Rugs and wedding blankets were her favorite things to weave. "The covers and rugs—they're the important ones," she says. After the festivities, the bride is wrapped in the blanket and is ushered to her new home. Fadma made these special items for each of her daughters' marriages and takes great pride in having given them as gifts. God would reward her for her work, she was sure.

Bridal blankets are typically striped, although the number and style of the stripes is up to the weaver. What matters most is that the blanket be exceptionally fine. "Parents want something rich, expensive, and pretty so they can show off their daughter in it."

Pile rugs contain more complicated designs, which means that weavers have to count the threads to make the patterns come out right. "It's the brain that works. Whatever design your eye sees, you have to figure out. You go over to some woman's house, you notice what she's doing, and you think about how to copy it." Sometimes Fadma borrows designs from her earlier rugs or from decorative elements on old buildings. Sometimes she creates a design from nature: a flower in the field or an insect's footprint.

The designs evolve as Fadma works at the loom. "As you're weaving, it becomes clear what you'll put in the rug. Even if you've already chosen the designs, you think about what you might add. The main thing is to make the rug pretty, to decorate it so that it will look really nice and everyone who sees it will say, 'What a good woman!'"

The dominant color of rugs from this arid area is a bright gold that they call apricot, which is used for the warp and the rows of filler between the knotted rows. Women weave several filler rows in between the knotted rows so the pile lies flat. These rugs are more lightweight than those with only one row of filler.

In her weaving days, after Fadma would choose the main color, she would select the compatible hues, perhaps brown with gray, red with black, or black with white. There is a local theory of colors in which one color is thought to "cool" the other. For example, red is hot, but green and white cool it. Aziza and her group of young weavers often discuss which colors go together, and if they're not

The decision to tattoo her chin and forehead, despite her husband's disapproval, is an outward symbol of Fadma's independence.

sure, they will ask someone older. "We always ask, and we always learn from them," she says.

When Fadma was ready to weave, she would send a man to buy a sack of wool at the Thursday market in Ouarzazate, a town about twenty kilometers away. She carded and spun the wool, sometimes mixing the black and white to make gray. Fadma calls it green, the

same hue as the grayish green leaves of the absinthe plant used to make tea in winter.

Dye plants are scarce in this desert environment, and so natural dyes have never been part of Fadma's repertoire. Instead she relies on chemical dyes along with aluminum chloride as a mordant. "Henna [a plant, which is natural and readily available here] is not my taste," she says.

Fadma used to weave year-round. Without taking a pause she'd finish a rug, cut it off, and immediately start another. All this she did in the quiet evenings and spare moments of the day when she wasn't cooking or gathering fodder for the mules, donkeys, and sheep.

Once a stranger appeared at the door and asked if he could weave alongside her. No one knew where he came from, but he was young and eager, and so Fadma agreed. They'd sit at the loom together and stay up late at night telling stories. Fadma's husband, children, and neighbors would join in, eating, drinking tea, and filling the house with laughter. "He knew how to weave as well as a woman," Aziza says. "People who were living then still talk about it."

Being able to weave is a basic skill expected of all village girls and women so they can furnish their homes; textiles are still the main furniture here in the far south. An excellent weaver may develop a wide reputation and sometimes achieve fame. Women look upon such a woman as wise and go to her for personal advice. People say, "There's no one like Fadma, she's the best."

As Fadma puts it, "Weaving gives you value, with people and with God. It's a blessing, like you did a good deed in the world. And because wool comes from nature, there is a blessing in it too." Fadma mentions that one design, a star with five points, is a symbol for the five daily prayers. For Fadma, weaving is a spiritual calling.

It also provides economic rewards. Unfortunately, the pricing of rugs often gets tangled up with gender dynamics. In Fadma's village, husbands set the sales price and seldom consult their wives. "The woman works the wool, washes and cards and spins, so she knows how much she's used. But the man doesn't ask, and he's really tough. He thinks he knows everything, he won't listen to you, and he makes the decisions. He says no one should talk, only him. He should control everything."

Weavers use a bright apricot color, *mishmashi*, for the warp and several filler rows between knotted rows.

Aziza sees beneath the surface. "It's because the man doesn't want to appear weak," she says. "He wants to make it look like he's the one who knows, he's the one in charge. If people heard him asking his wife how much time she worked on a rug, they'd say he was afraid of his wife. I've seen it many times. If a man helps his wife fetch water, people say, 'His wife bosses him around. Where did she get that magic spell?'"

But Fadma is the sort of woman who didn't always obey. One day she decided to have her chin, forehead, and left wrist tattooed. Considered fashionable fifty years ago, facial tattoos were usually a kitchen operation, done by untrained women using a sewing needle and black soot from a cooking pot.

Fadma and her husband were friends with another couple in the army, and once when the men went off, the other woman offered to give Fadma a tattoo. At first Fadma resisted. "My husband will get mad at me," she said, but the friend insisted. Knowing her husband would be angry, she still went ahead and had it done, all three tattoos in one day. They didn't hurt much, but later Fadma broke out in a fever. Her husband came home to find her in bed and asked what was the matter. He couldn't see because she'd covered her face.

"But the next morning my friend came by and woke me up. It was then he saw my face and shouted, 'What did you do? Did you want to pretty yourself up?' I told him that I wanted it, and it was what God wanted for me. 'And besides,' I said, 'I was already pretty, without the tattoos.' It's true; I was really pretty, and strong and healthy, and I had big eyes. I was a beauty." Although now she is old and almost blind, she still looks for the positive: "I'm always with people; I get together with them and enjoy them."

Despite her independent streak, Fadma's husband usually dealt with the outside world. He'd take her rugs to the weekly market or to shops in the nearby town. Nowadays Fadma's daughters sell their rugs on their own, and when tourists come to the village, Aziza and her friends take their work to the women's association and sometimes travel to craft exhibitions in larger towns. But it was different in the old days. "He didn't tell me how much my rugs sold for, and I didn't ask. If I said something, he'd hit me. Give me

Above: Fadma sits next to her granddaughter Aziza at home along with other family members. Left: A *hemel,* a large flatwoven piece used to cover the floor.

money? God knows, I didn't get a thing. He said, 'You eat and you drink, you and your kids. I'm the one who has to run around and earn.' And it wasn't just me; the whole village was like that. But in fact, my work earned more than his. I took care of the cattle, sheep, goats, and chickens, which I could always sell. And I wove. He grew wheat and hard wheat, but he didn't sell them; the family ate them." With her weaving income, Fadma earned enough to buy a metal loom in 2001, which her family uses and she loans out free of charge, a service that will surely earn her blessings.

At one time, Fadma's husband ran a sideline that has since disappeared. Living on the edge of the Sahara Desert, with old trading caravans passing through, Fadma's family entertained a stream of guests, and many beggars, too. "People who sold charcoal, people with trucks of salt, he'd put the sellers together with buyers. He knew how to talk the villagers into buying things they didn't know

they needed. Now they don't care if things come or not. If they need something, they go to the market. People still say, 'When Si Abderrahaman died, everything went from this village.' Even the beggars don't come here anymore."

Fadma doesn't take into account her husband's profits from "putting people together" or his military pension. But when all is tallied up, she was the main breadwinner of the family, as other women often are today.

Fadma's life is exceptional because, along with her notable career as a weaver, she has traveled widely and enjoyed many adventures. Yet she's also maintained traditional beliefs and family ties, as exemplified by her loving relationship with her granddaughter Aziza. Married at twelve and still indomitable, Fadma reveals the strength of character bequeathed by the older generation of Moroccan women.

VANISHING TRADITIONS

ALTHOUGH FATIMA FDIL GREW UP in a lush landscape, her life, and the place of weaving in it, reflects the stresses and strains endured by older weavers. She used to live in a tent from March to December, tending the family's sheep as they grazed in the surrounding meadows. "I'd cook the food, watch the sheep, haul water from the spring, weave. I'd carry food to the farmworkers at our house. It was a long way, and I had my daughter and son on my back. See how much I worked? I got exhausted. I did it until I couldn't do it anymore."

Fatima was born in the village of Ben Smim, nestled in a beautiful green valley at the heart of the Middle Atlas Mountains. Her future husband was born in the same village, but he inherited some land, and when she married him, she moved to his nearby farm. She was only thirteen but was already capable of taking care of a home.

"We used to get married very young in those days. Now you finish high school and then get married. Here they married us off and we didn't know anything. What are you going to do? When your father gives you in marriage, you have to go. Not like today, when a girl gives herself on her own or even says no."

Her husband, Moulay Abderrahaman, was a widower with a young son and daughter, **Fatima Lrhachi** (page 28). Fatima went on to have six children of her own. One son and three daughters survived, including the youngest, **Habiba Lrhachi,** a college graduate who lives a radically different life in Tangier

(page 83). After the other children left home, Fatima and her husband continued to share their home with their grown son and his family and share in the farming and household chores. "I farm, weave, cook, wash, make bread, take care of the children. All at the same time. Today and tomorrow. Always. That's what I do."

Fatima's husband is a *sherif*, a descendant of the Prophet Muhammad, and Fatima is a *sherifa*. The couple is well respected, and because of their status and moral character are often called upon to settle disputes. Fatima possesses a natural dignity and faith, as well as simplicity and warmth, that underlie her life as a weaver.

Fatima has been weaving since she was a girl sitting by her mother's side. "If I hadn't watched her, how would I have learned? I memorized it. When I came to my own house, my husband had no furnishings. My mother came and helped me set up the loom. In a year, I knew everything."

Fatima produces all the styles that distinguish her village's rich weaving tradition, from knotted rugs and flatweaves, both plain striped and decorated, to throw pillows and plain wool blankets. Flatweaves embellished with delicate allover designs and sequins are the most difficult and technically demanding pieces, and true to character, these are the rugs Fatima prefers to make. "It's pretty enough for a bride to hang on the wall and have her picture taken in front of it." She also makes clothing like men's jellabas and women's capes, both the small fine ones and the larger ones decorated with sequins.

Farmland near Fatima's home.

Fatima and her blankets and rugs.

a design wider than the others and woven with a unique pattern. There should be six stripes on either side of the center, each different from the others, but matching the stripe in the same position on the other side of the center. Further, the stripes should get wider as they approach the central stripe, which will run down the middle of a woman's back when she wears the cape. These textiles are worked vertically and with the non-design side facing the weaver. The first six stripes are rolled up when the next six are done, so the weaver must remember all the designs and how they are placed.

"This work is really hard," Fatima admits. "The majority of women here in the village aren't educated, but they make these complicated things. Your mind tells you what to do."

Weaving also requires a great deal of physical labor. To begin with, Fatima processes her own wool from the sheep she raises. She spins the warp and weft threads separately, because the warp needs to be tighter and stronger. She also dyes her own wool, using commercial dyes purchased in the nearby town of Azrou. "I take red dye, put it in water, add a little salt, and cook it over the fire, then add wool and stir it so the yarn doesn't burn." To ensure that the wool won't fade in the sun, she uses this process and gives it a good wash with Tide.

It's afternoon and time to start weaving. "You need to work on wool, even if you don't have time. You make lunch early in the morning, milk the cow, make bread, and churn the buttermilk. After lunch, you weave from about one o'clock to five, when you have a snack. Then you bring in the sheep and make dinner. That's what we do.

"When you're ready to begin a rug, you say the declaration of faith, the first pillar of Islam, 'There is only one God and Muhammad is His Prophet,' and when you finish the rug, you do the same. Your weaving acquires a soul when you start winding the warp. Before you take it off the loom, you give it a drink of water. You put the metal beater in a little salted water, repeat the declaration of faith three times, and then you cut it off. You do that because the weaving has a soul, like us. (Muslims say the same phrase when they are about to die, if they are able.)

"During Ramadan, working wool is especially nice. It's like worshipping God. You wake up early, tidy your house, fetch water, do dishes, get everything ready. You're fasting and happy. Some

One of those pieces that she's proud of is a finely woven woman's cape made of her softest wool. A good woman's cape will have designs in colored stripes separated by white wool plain weave, sometimes accented with thin lines of white cotton or rayon. On the back of the striped design are tufted rows of white cotton or rayon, providing an alternate pattern so the cape can be worn on either side. Fatima notes that the cape should have a central stripe with

women card wool, some women weave. We laugh and play until three. Then we make bread and soup and fried bread. Each one does her job. It's good when the women get together and weave during Ramadan."

Being a good weaver, and being good at all her work, will enhance a woman's value. But if she's not good in this way, people will laugh at her or not respect her. Apart from this and the artistic and spiritual rewards, weaving offers Fatima's family a host of practical comforts. "It gives you furnishings for the house. You provide rugs for your children so they don't get cold. In the past, we didn't have banquettes to sit and sleep on. We used rugs. Oh, how much I wove! I filled the house with them! You slept on rugs or blankets on the floor. You needed them for the children, the people who helped with the harvest, the shepherds, you and your husband, guests. You had to have bedding for them all."

In addition to furnishing her home, Fatima sometimes puts her rugs up for sale. Because she doesn't feel confident enough to market them, her worldly daughter Habiba sets the price and places them on the Internet. Occasionally Fatima sells to tourists visiting her home, and once in a while her husband takes the rugs to the weekly outdoor market in nearby Azrou where he sells them to a middleman.

The village of Ben Smim and surrounding farmland.

Like those of many women, Fatima's rugs serve as a kind of savings account; she sells one when she needs money. Now that she and her husband are getting too old for heavy farmwork, they are more dependent on rug sales to cover food and basic household expenses. Fortunately, their youngest son has a job and helps his parents financially. In a dramatic change from the past, their working daughter, Habiba, contributes as well. This trend, for girls to have jobs and contribute to the family, has led to a decrease in the parental preference for sons.

Fatima notes the generational differences, which you can see in her own family. "Girls today, there aren't many who weave. They work in gardens, at the summer camp, or in co-ops. They don't sit at home in front of the loom. I worked in my own gardens, but I wove too. Now working in the communal gardens pays money. And now wives help their husbands. Now everyone works. Men

Left: A *tarhalt*, used to decorate the walls at weddings.
Below: Fatima, husband, son Khalid, and grandchild.

Fatima at her loom, the traditional style made of wood.

and women are the same; they work to eat. It used to be that a woman would finish a rug every four or five days and then start another. Now they go off and work in agriculture, planting onions or squash and weeding the government's wheat fields.

"I taught my four daughters how to weave. My youngest, Habiba, went to university. Fatima went to grade school. The two older girls didn't go to school at all. If Habiba had stayed here, ai yi yi, you can just imagine what she would make! And Zuhor, if she had stayed, but her place is too small for a loom. My daughter who lives on a military base does have a loom set up. All my daughters like to weave when they have time."

"That's true," says the one daughter who never left home. "The fact is, more girls in Ben Smim would weave if it were profitable."

"There are plenty of machine-made blankets at the market," Fatima adds. "In the past, we didn't have those, or foam rubber mattresses, just what we wove. But these days, work has taken the young women away from this kind of life. Only a few old ladies still weave."

FATIMA LRHACHI

FOLLOWING THE ANCESTORS

IT'S HARD TO KNOW WHY some people leave and some people stay in the place where they were born. Whatever the reasons, Fatima Lrhachi is one of the few who maintains the weaving traditions of Ben Smim. She grew up among hills of wild lavender and groves of cherry and pomegranate trees. For years her husband supported her and their five children by growing wheat, peas, tomatoes, and potatoes until he was too old to work. Now she lives in a house in the village furnished with electricity, running water, and a television set. She has a cell phone and access to the Internet. Otherwise her life is not much different from her stepmother's, Fatima Fdil (page 22).

The house accommodates three generations of family members: her twenty-year-old son; her single daughter, who holds a degree in economics; and her married daughter, son-in-law, and their small son. Following the current trend, two of Fatima's daughters went off to work in the big city. None of the daughters weave. "School took them, and I felt sorry. A craft is an important thing. But they didn't have the time to learn." The extended family depends on Fatima's earnings.

"I began weaving when I was fourteen. My paternal aunt, God rest her soul, started me off with a little flatweave pillow. 'Do like this, do like that,' she said." Seven years later, she was expert enough to weave large flatweaves. She remembers the year because she wove the date on her first big rug.

Soon Fatima's five small children were taking up all her time. But when they got older and needed money for books, transporta-

Left: Fatima Lrhachi carries on the weaving traditions of the Middle Atlas village of Ben Smim.
Opposite: Detail of a large flatweave rug.

tion, tennis shoes, and other school expenses, she began weaving again. Now she weaves full-time, except when she's hired to cook at an agricultural camp or pick peas in the fields. "When it's cold, and there's nothing to do, that's when I work wool." Though her daughters sometimes help, she prefers to work alone.

Not too long ago, Fatima did some weaving with women in a new cooperative in the village. They supplied her with enough wool to make a checkerboard rug, but when she finished weaving it, she never went back. "I'd say, 'You do it this way,' and they'd say, 'You do it that way.' When you're weaving, you have to really care about it and give it your full attention. It has to be symmetrical, with each knot in the right place and the warp done right. Their

work had holes as big as caves! Well, are you going to keep fighting with people? I saw their work. I didn't like it and I left."

Fatima produces all the styles typical of the Middle Atlas area. Here men's jellabas are made of brown wool adorned with a white snowflake design and sometimes touches of indigo blue. Women's jellabas are made of store-bought fabric, but the women's capes are woven of wool, cotton, or rayon thread and decorated with sequins for celebrations.

For the home, Fatima continues to make wool pillows that will decorate the low banquettes in the living room. She also makes rag rugs from pieces of old clothing, which, like American quilts, hold family memories. Her flatweave rugs contain an overall geometric

design rather than the alternating stripes that are also common in this area. These masterpieces of complex patterns are woven from the back and decorated with sequins. They are taken out for parties, weddings, or national holidays. If used every day, moisture would dull or rust the expensive sequins. "Everything has its use. Everything serves. You make what the house needs. The living room may need a rug a certain size, or the in-laws may come to visit and you need blankets for them. Or if a man needs a jellaba and his wife is a weaver, what will people say if he has nothing to wear?"

She considers a jellaba she made for her husband as her best work. It combined natural black wool and a white yarn with seeds in it. "It was pretty, and it looked good on my husband, but I needed money so the kids could go to school. I didn't want to sell it. My sister Habiba sold it to a professor at the university. I got a good price, but it left an empty spot."

Fatima doesn't work from a pattern as do weavers in commercial workshops in the big cities. Nor does she follow the general style of her region. In fact, there is no longer a characteristic style. Greater mobility and intermarriage have ushered in a wider variety of local styles and a wider range of designs. With so much to choose from, Fatima has never made the same rug twice. "In the end, it's you and your ideas," she says.

As creative as she is, Fatima is nevertheless a stickler for detail. "When you start weaving, you have a plan. You say, 'I'm going to put the border here, and I'll put this design here and I'll count, I'll figure out the middle.' The important thing is that you focus on the center, so that the rug will be symmetrical. If you drew a picture and didn't focus on the center, it would come out crooked, wouldn't it? A rug is like a picture."

When it comes to color, Fatima has to depend on what dyes are available. "You choose a color that will go with the others, that doesn't fade or rub off on your clothes. You wash the yarn after you dye it, and soak it in vinegar so it won't run. Blue doesn't run, and also red, so I set those colors myself. Henna leaves produce a rust color. Madder root for maroon, tree bark for brown can be found in the wild." But the spread of private property has dimin-

This rug, measuring about 5 x 3 1/2 feet, took three women seven days to weave.

ished communal lands and the availability of dye plants. "If the owner of the forest catches you, you're in trouble."

"But weaving prevents you from gossiping, right? You stay home and do your work and mind your own business. Also our religion tells you, 'A craft, though it doesn't make you rich, shelters and protects you.' You can clothe yourself and your children with your own hands. There's nothing better than that.

"The important thing is you're addicted to work. If you're addicted to the work, if you have a craft as a calling, you manage to get the wool and dyes and supplies you need."

Fortune smiles when people give her sheep fleeces as gifts. The quality of this wool is as good as or better than the wool sold at the souk. "You go to the market and look. Your eye is your measure. You save the nice white for special things like a jellaba or flatweave rug. You sort it into three or four different kinds. And what's not good enough, you dye or have dyed. Souk wool spun

Fatima spins wool when she is tired from weaving, but she is always working with wool.

into yarn can have moths, not like the wool from home that you've been taking care of."

If Fatima is feeling good, she weaves. If she's worn out, she spins. When she gets an online order from the United States via marrakeshexpress.org or theanou.com, she works on it as much as she can.

Fatima sets the prices for her rugs, though it's hard to keep track of her time and expenses. It takes all day just to card half a kilo of wool. A kilo of processed wool costs $7.90 in the market, and dyeing costs $1.90 a kilo. The small red rug seen on page 30 took seven days for three co-op women to weave, a total of three weeks of labor. Then there's the cost of the trips into town for dyeing, to drop off and pick up the wool, and to the post office. "I can't count it all. You just estimate. If you went to add it all up, well, you wouldn't work wool again."

Fatima used to sell her rugs at the weekly market in Azrou. Now she depends on orders from my website where she and her rugs are featured along with others in the village. She has yet to receive orders from friends or relatives who live in cities and do not weave.

When it comes down to it, Fatima's stints as a cook and field-worker provide more money than weaving. How, then, does she support herself, her husband, two daughters, and a son, son-in-law, and grandson? Without the son-in-law's contribution, the family would starve.

According to Fatima, weaving fails to improve a woman's social status or reputation. "Long ago they used to say, 'Get a wife who can dress you and her children.' Now people want blankets for the lowest possible price. Work with wool isn't valued anymore."

Fatima is facing a worldwide problem: competition with cheap, factory-made goods. People want manufactured blankets made of polar fleece. They buy floor mats made of plastic. The increasingly popular "Turkish rugs" are made by machine somewhere in Turkey and Belgium and smuggled in or brought as gifts by family members working in Europe. Moroccans like them because they are lightweight and easier to shake out and wash than a heavy handmade rug.

"I feel bad. Wool costs a lot, and you have to wash, card, spin, dye, and weave it. People say they'll buy machine-made blankets for $10. At $90, mine in wool would still be cheap. I'm willing to weave for someone who really wants one 'from her heart,' because that person will pay a good price.

"Right now, very few know how to work wool. Even if you want someone to help you, they won't know how. Hardly any young people weave. The young are finished. Education took them. They sit at the computer all day. Are they going to card wool? It's not possible."

One major reason is that there are no economic incentives. If young women got good prices, they would be encouraged to weave. But no one can survive on one order every year or two.

"Well, there's still a small group that makes rugs. We'll have to wait a while and see what happens. If there's no weaving and no income from it, people will have to figure out another way to manage. They'd have to go back to zero. That's why we need to encourage the young women on their computers to learn weaving. Otherwise the craft will die out."

Opposite Left: The front and back of a rag rug made from recycled unraveled sweaters.
Opposite Right: A brown jellaba, a style that often has a white snowflake design scattered on it. A few also have touches of blue, which may be indigo.
Right: Fatima's handspun wool.

THE RUG SELLER OF KHEMISSET

WEAVERS WHO CANNOT SELL THEIR WORK, no matter how fine, face an uncertain future. Few women have access to shops and markets or possess the savvy it takes to deal in a male-dominated profession. Aicha Duha is the exception: years ago she made a giant leap into the man's world and became a middlewoman. She buys rugs from rural women and sells them to merchants or private clients in Khemisset and Rabat. In breaks between the buyers and sellers crowded around her rug stall, Aicha, her sister Yemmas, and I took tea and talked about her career.

"I used to be a weaver. I worked morning, noon, and night. If I didn't work for a week, I wouldn't have anything to eat. I got sick with the 'nerves' from all the work. And so I started to buy and sell to earn a little something. Thank God, I make enough to live on." That was twenty years ago. Since then she's become an expert on rug quality and a trailblazing entrepreneur.

Aicha was born in a small village near Khemisset, a busy market town in a rich agricultural area about an hour's drive from the capital of Rabat. She never attended school and has never married. She shares a house with her sister Yemmas, who has two sons in their thirties. When Yemmas was pregnant with the younger son, her husband disappeared and they have not heard from him since. "He left. We don't ask about him, and he doesn't ask about us." The sons have a grade school education and a fitful record of odd jobs in construction. Aicha is the main support for herself and her sister's family.

"Hard work showed me how to weave; that, and watching the neighbor women. I didn't have anything and I needed to work." Three years later, Aicha was earning money making pile rugs and flatweaves, especially the local Khemisset and Tifelt styles.

The all-wool Khemisset rugs have a red ground with designs in black, white, and gold or orange. Traditionally, these designs are less complex than the Tifelt rugs (see below). They also come in smaller sizes (2 x 3 feet or 2 x 5 feet), which appeal to tourists drawn to the colorful weekly market.

Opposite: Woven all in wool with a red ground, this Khemisset style rug features black, white, and orange resembling the fields of poppies and orange flowers here in the spring.
Right: Tifelt style rugs often use a blue ground with intricate designs.

Tifelt rugs often have a blue ground, unusual in Moroccan rugs, and the designs are more intricate. In addition to wool, they use rayon thread (*sabra*), which makes the designs finer.

Some weavers combine the two styles. Rugs might include col-

A beautiful example of Khemisset color combined with the Tifelt palette and designs.

ors from the Khemisset palette as well as the more complex Tifelt designs in the wide bands. The deep red background is typical of rugs from Khemisset and Zemmour. The rare knotted rugs from Zemmour borrow the Khemisset colors: a red ground with

black, white, and gold accents. Usually the surface design is done in squares, which is seldom seen in Moroccan rugs outside the south. These rugs can be used on either side, knotted or pile side up for warmth in the winter, and flat side up in the summer. Other Zemmour rugs have an overall design with central medallions and a border.

Aicha used to make knotted rugs, but they were not her favorite. "Knotted rugs are really hard. You knot and cut with a knife, knot and cut with a knife. With a Khemisset flatweave, the thread just keeps going."

Yemmas agrees. "There are simple designs and there are complex ones. One style goes quickly and the other keeps your hands busy and takes more time."

Aicha says the blue Tifelt rugs are also hard to make. "And if you use a Tifelt design in a Khemisset rug, it's really difficult."

The rayon thread used for the Tifelt style is sometimes called silk (*hrir*). Aicha once worked with real silk, but it's now expensive and hard to find. Today even rayon costs more than the most expensive wool. The cheapest wool, which costs about $4 a kilo, has thorns and seeds in it and needs to be cleaned and combed. Warps used to be made from this tougher wool, but now most weavers purchase ready-made yarn. It looks like cotton, and they say it is cotton and "plastic" spun together, or it may be rayon combined with polyester for strength.

Since the colors of the Khemisset and Tifelt rugs are traditional, Aicha didn't need to choose them, but she did choose the designs. As with other Middle Atlas flatweaves, there are rules in applying those designs. "I did that work by measuring so the design would be the same at the other end." Only one design area is not repeated, and that is the central stripe in a striped design. The designs have names, and according to Aicha, refer to something from nature or daily life. There are various ways of creating and adapting these designs.

Eight years ago, Aicha wove her last rug and began selling full-time. "I saw that my craft didn't get me anywhere. I couldn't get by on what I earned. I had to change with the times. Now, thank God, I get by on my earnings."

"I went around selling my rugs at the market and I watched. I wanted to copy the middlemen, to buy and sell like them. Even

Aicha in her stall with a variety of Khemisset and Tifelt rugs.

though I didn't have money for much stock, I bought what I could. I wasn't a real merchant, I just did the little I could manage. I would circulate through the market with my rugs over my arm." Now that she's acquired a permanent stall in Khemisset, business has improved.

The problem is she has no storage space in Khemisset and has to carry her rugs back and forth every Tuesday. Every Monday and Thursday she travels to the rug auction and outdoor market in Rabat. There she has storage but no covered stall. She does get a ride with a friend, and once a week Yemmas comes along. She'd help more often, but the trip costs $15 for them both. "When the market begins, I just sit in the street and hope to sell something. If I don't, I take my rugs back to the shop where I store them. Sometimes I sell a piece, sometimes nothing. Every day, it's just your luck. I don't count my time sitting there and waiting for a customer. The important thing is I make enough to get by."

She and her sister own a two-story home in a nice neighborhood. To buy, it they sold rugs and borrowed from family. They've since paid back the loan little by little, no mean accomplishment for two women on their own. Aicha bears the full weight of the household expenses on her shoulders. Although she is a shrewd businesswoman in other regards, she spends the money as it comes in and doesn't seem to keep track. Or perhaps she didn't want to say.

"Right now, weaving is slow. There aren't many buyers, so we're not selling. But people are still working. Really they have no alternative. They don't get paychecks, so they have to weave. Remember, any kind of honest work is part of our religious life. If a woman weaves and uses the money to buy something to eat, she's living *halal*, following the acceptable way.

"It's also said that if a woman is a good weaver, it will improve her chances of marriage. She can work for herself and for her husband. She'd help out." But so far Aicha hasn't won a husband,

Aicha with an array of gorgeous rugs in her stall at the Khemisset market.

although she's been engaged twice. She ended the first relationship because her fiancé didn't have a good job. The second candidate was an African-American Muslim who left Morocco after their engagement party and never returned. "It wasn't meant to be," she says. Nevertheless, she would still like to marry. "He should be Muslim or willing to become Muslim. He could be from any country, no problem. I'd like to live in another country if it's fated.

He just has to be honest. If he marries me, he shouldn't divorce me; he should stay with me always. I don't want marriage to be taken lightly. I want it to be permanent.

"A woman always lives in difficult conditions. She needs someone to help her. A woman alone gets worn out. If she has housework, she needs someone working outside to provide for her. If she also works outside, like me, she has two jobs. But what can you do? My work has taught me patience, thank God."

A Gallery of Middle Atlas Rugs

SOMETIMES I DESCRIBE MIDDLE ATLAS rugs as going from limited design layouts—even just plain stripes in blankets—to horizontal alternate colored and design stripes like the Zemmour rugs, to stripes with a lacy overlay, to an overall design.

Large Zemmour rug

Red ground with gold, black, and white designs, flatweave. These rugs are called Zemmour after the tribal confederation in the area where they are made. The market town in that area is Khemisset, about an hour and a half inland, east of Rabat, so sometimes they are called Khemisset rugs. Aicha Duha (page 34) sells this kind of rug at the weekly Tuesday market in Khemisset, and also in Rabat.

This large rug is an excellent example of this genre of weaving. The colors are rich, and the design both regular and complex. In a good rug of this type, each of the design bands is bordered by two identical bands in another design, as shown here. The large areas of red in this rug highlight the finely woven motifs.

The warp and weft are all wool, except for the white, which is a cotton-like material (but may be rayon). Today many rugs are made with a synthetic weft, and wool weft is highly valued.

It is very difficult to date Moroccan rugs. I have had this rug for at least twenty-five years, and it was not new when purchased. You rarely find such finely-woven rugs now. It may be thirty to fifty years old, or more.

Middle Atlas flatweave

Colorful plain stripes, complex design bands, and limited white overlay.

This rug is all wool, warp and weft, except for the white, which is probably rayon or cotton. It is probably from the Beni Mtir area, north and east of Azrou, where they use a lot of blue.

This is a masterpiece of weaving; note the complex motifs in the design bands. It also has the regularity of a central band bordered by mirroring motif bands whose small border bands also match. Except at one end, two extra design bands are added, one very complex, the other rather simple. There is a small white design woven into the border near the central band—it may have been the marker for the center. Perhaps the rug was not long enough, and the weaver added extra designs. The design at the very end matches that at the start, so it is not a fragment. The plain-colored stripes also mirror each other near the center of the rug, but vary more toward the ends.

The white overlay on the edges is the same general design, but the small diamonds within it don't match across the rug. The lattice is in three vertical rows; it does not cross the design bands, and it skips some of the colored stripe areas, too.

The main colors are a pale cherry red, indigo blue, and violet, often found in rugs just east of the Beni Mtir area. Seeing the blue and violet and white pattern yarns on the back of a rug always makes me want to see the front; it's bound to be good. There are highlights in orange and a soft green.

Middle Atlas flatweave rug

Horizontal and vertical designs with bright color bands.

This rug is from the area around Azrou, perhaps the Beni Mtir area a bit to the north. The colors on the back are brighter, so it has faded in the light. The warp and weft are wool except for the white in the design stripes, which may be cotton or rayon.

This rug has the symmetry that local weavers told me about in their capes for women: there is a center, and on each side symmetrical designs mirroring each other. This piece is unusual in several ways. For one, the center design is split in two, with each half mirroring the other. As one moves out, the design stripes on each side mirror each other—almost. The way they don't is only in the diamonds in the center of those design stripes: they vary in size, color, and design; one side has dots in the center of the diamonds. We see variation again in the next design stripes near the ends. Each has a theme of diamonds with borders—but look closely. The designs within the diamonds are very different, as are the designs along their edges. Colors vary too, with a red "outline" in one and a violet one in the other. This is one reason I love Middle Atlas rugs: you can look and look and keep seeing new things.

The plain stripes are more regular. There is a sequence of blue, cherry red, black, orange, and what I call "self-destruct violet," probably the aniline dye fuchsine because it fades a lot. All the stripes are "linked" with notches of their color into the next color band. This is true of color except for the stripes between the two center design bands where the black is replaced by green, and there is a thin violet stripe within the red. Also, there is just one pattern that "links" the color bands.

The lacy vertical bands are also regular in their pattern, with all three rows having "toothed" diamonds with either a closed or a "line" diamond in the center; these center diamonds alternate. Each row has two borders, and those at the edge of the rug are like the fishbone pattern. The others are series of full and truncated filled-in diamonds. The lacy bands are laid over the colored stripes but visually go under the design stripes.

The overall effect is a beautiful rug that looks rather simple but is built on complex elements.

Middle Atlas long violet rug with lacy design overlay

This rug is all wool, warp and weft and even the white designs. The wool softens them and makes them stand out less than in the previous rug. The mauve color is found in rugs from the eastern part of the Middle Atlas. You can see the many color variations, probably both in dye batch and uneven fading. It's probably an aniline dye, the fuchsine that fades quickly. The green and yellow may be natural dyes and the blue indigo. The delicate touches of pink are not bright like most aniline dyes.

The design is somewhat like the previous rug. The design stripes are less symmetrical in their patterning; not all mirror each other. Most are confined to or define a clear strip, but in the seond row from the top one bursts out of the boundaries. White diamonds are scattered in the plain color bands, and their distribution seems somewhat symmetrical, though not regular, throughout the rug. The plain stripes are in very different, muted colors, giving this rug a visual softness.

The lacy white overlay differs from the following rugs in that here it lies over all parts of the rug, both the plain and design bands. It is also less symmetrical. Each vertical band has different figures; the overlay interrupts the designs. It looks as if there are butterflies fluttering up the central column. However, the edges of these vertical rows are all the same, in the fishbone pattern.

Middle Atlas flatweave with overall design bands

This rug comes from the Azrou area, where one often finds this overall design without plain-colored strips. It is probably from the Beni Mguild area, south of Azrou. The rug is all wool, warp and weft, except for the strips of bright white rows that are knotted, found in rugs from this area, but not very often. There are five bands of an identical design, which is usually found in borders; in a sense, they do serve as borders to the other design areas in this rug. The four main design areas include two similar, but not identical, chevrons at the ends. The other two main design areas use diamonds, but in different ways. The brown ground is very attractive to Westerners, who sometimes shy away from bright colors. There are color accents in orange, pink, mauve, and green, the latter turned tan on the rug's face.

THE WEAVERS OF N'KOB

FAR TO THE SOUTH, SCHOOLING and jobs are less available than in Khemisset. Yet the weavers of N'kob enjoy a better market and better sales, which encourage young women to practice, and actively promote, their weaving tradition.

N'kob lies in the ragged foothills of the Anti-Atlas Mountains, an isolated village of stone houses near the end of a road that winds south from Marrakesh over the snowcapped peaks of the High Atlas Mountains, crosses green plains, blooming with pink oleander, and climbs through fields and orchards miraculously terraced in rocky terrain. The landscape is spectacular, but before the paved road was built three years ago, the village was almost lost to the rest of the world. The nearest town, Tazenakht, was a hard day's walk away. Even now this busy market center is a forty-minute drive, and since public transportation is virtually nonexistent, women rarely go there. The weavers of N'kob produce some of the finest rugs in Morocco, and weaving from this area is respected all over Morocco and beyond. The knotted rugs from this area are called "Tazenakht," or "High Atlas," or "Ait Ouzgite," and come from the famous Jebel Siroua weaving area.

N'kob contains a mix of peoples. Its 800 inhabitants are either descendants of fair-skinned nomads or black Africans who socialize but seldom intermarry. There are several areas like this in Morocco, some of which included Berber-speaking Jews, and they are accurately referred to as an ethnic mosaic. Yet everyone speaks Berber and everyone ekes out a living from the soil or from herding. Although the surrounding mountains are arid and the sheep seem to graze on stones, a fresh stream irrigates the wheat fields and almond trees. The income is rarely enough, and as a result, the men often go off to work construction in the big cities, leaving the women behind.

In fact, most families depend on women's weavings to make ends meet. Luckily, weavers have access to a good market offering steady sales.

Actually the market comes to them. Most women are reluctant to sell at the weekly souk in Tazenakht, mainly because they need a middleman to carry the rug around and get bids on it, and he'll take part of the profit. Dealing with shopkeepers is no better. The stores lining the main street of Tazenakht, all with colorful rugs hanging out front to tempt buyers, advertise themselves as cooperatives, but only use that label to entice sympathetic tourists. Usually the rugs are on consignment, and the weavers are not paid until the rug sells. Weavers dislike this system and prefer receiving cash payments by selling directly to a middleman who comes to the house, which he will do for a good weaver. As Anaya Seqqat says, "We haggle over the price. Sometimes we don't agree and he leaves, and another one will come." These middlemen sell the rugs to higher-level middlemen who take them to stores in Marrakesh. The situation is not ideal, but it does get them a better

Aicha and Anaya Seqqat's mother and Fadma Buhassi and Ijja Id Ali Boufkir's grandmother holds prickly broom used to make yellow dye.

price and spare them the hassle of spending a full day away from home and sitting in the hot sun waiting for a sale. Besides, it gives women some control over their work.

The village produces a wide variety of textiles, and most weavers make several types of products to increase the chance of a sale.

Rugs

Iklan literally means "design" and generally refers to a type of flatwoven rug that incorporates particular symbols.

Chedwi is a two-sided design combined with a black and white flatweave and twining technique, rarely made today. The colors in these rugs are often produced from natural dyes.

Tarz or **teereera** is an old style, seen in the patterned stripes of some antique chedwis, and is currently being revived. The geometric designs are the same on the front and the back, a technique that is complex and hard to weave. One woman suggested that teereera literally means "back and forth," which is what you do when weaving this design.

Bu tilwah ("*picture*" rug) is a flatweave with squares containing different designs like little pictures, or like the wooden tablets students used to write on in Quranic school, sometimes separated by borders in pile.

Terz is a relatively new flatweave style called "embroidery," which it resembles.

Glaoui are rugs named after a local warlord of the early twentieth century and are distinctive for combining three weaving techniques: pile, flatweave, and twining.

N'kob, nestled in the rugged Anti-Atlas mountains.

Left: Terz rug with bu tilwah squares.
Right: A rug in the style of teereera with chedwi, meaning a colored, two-sided design combined with the black and white flatweave and twining. The colors in such rugs were often from natural dyes.

Tahabant are simple flatweaves with small knotted designs in different colors scattered across a gray background. These are said to be in revival.

Kharita (*map*) or **bu idraran** (*mountains*) are flatweaves and consist of many varied small designs in one piece, often curved so they resemble mountains. Or they may resemble the maps women see in their children's schoolbooks. They are relatively recent and difficult to make because the pattern keeps changing and is the same on both faces.

Iboli are knotted or pile rugs composed of three or five central panels, all in geometric patterns, and surrounded by several borders. The rows of pile have rows of weft between them, so the rugs are less dense and lighter than knotted rugs from the northern cities of Rabat and Fes.

Traditional clothing

Tahaykt (women's capes) The traditional capes worn by N'kob women on special occasions are large rectangles of natural, cream-colored wool with intricate designs scattered along the edges. In the past, they were very long but are now only six feet or less in length.

Aghlaf (long bags) The long bags, woven in the two-sided *tarz* style, were made for men, but are seldom used today.

Ishkjid (boot panels) These woven panels, attached to leather

Left: A bu idraran (mountains) rug.
Right: A man carries his aghlaf.

soles and worn outdoors, also used the two-sided *tarz* pattern and style of weaving. The designs are fine and complex. They are not used today.

Hezam *(women's belts)* Women's woolen belts were finely woven in the *teereera* style in varied widths and worn folded in half. They are now extremely rare. Kebira Aglaou (page 74) recently tried to copy her mother's old belt, and it's interesting to see the difference between old and new.

The small patterns on these traditional articles of clothing are made with naturally dyed raw wool or yarn, a practice that has largely disappeared elsewhere in Morocco. Red is made from madder root, black from iron filings, pale yellow from prickly broom flowers, and golden yellow from apple tree bark. Walnut bark produces brown, and henna leaves a reddish brown. For a vivid blue,

women use indigo in a powder form combined with henna leaves, coal, or soot, and something sweet like dates or figs. Green results from a mixture of prickly broom yellow and indigo.

There's a science to it and an infinite number of variables, which have led to a decline in the use of natural dyes. For one thing, the plants are not always available in the wild. For another, it's a difficult and time-consuming process. First, weavers have to find the plant or flower, chop and mash it, then soak it in water for a few days before they can use it. After they drop the wool or yarn in the pot, anything can go wrong and will if they're not careful.

As it is, good-quality synthetic dyes are available in the market and in a tiny shop in the village. Weavers take the same care when

Left: Examples of women's belts, finely woven in wool, the left an antique and the right a modern copy.
Right: Detail of a traditional cape worn by women in N'kob.

using these commercial dyes, a feature that makes N'kob rugs so outstanding, in comparison with others using commercially dyed wool with its flat, uniform colors.

Weather affects the dyeing process, and seasons determine the time to weave. Like many women, Anaya Seqqat doesn't weave much during the spring when she has to gather fodder to feed the cows and sheep. Winter is another slow time of year for dyeing. It's hard to dye colors in winter because wool takes a long time to dry. Besides, it's difficult for women to sit and weave for long hours when the house is cold and the snow piles up to the door here in the mountains.

No one weaves on the Sabbath, which is Friday in Morocco, or during religious holidays, the month of Ramadan, and the ten days surrounding three major religious holidays: the Feast of the Sacrifice, the Prophet's birthday, and the Muslim New Year. The ten-day New Year's celebration is not so much a solemn occasion devoted to prayers and ceremonies as it is a time for entertaining friends and relatives and men returning from construction work in the big cities. It is a joyous holiday, and a true vacation, especially in southern Morocco.

The rest of the time, rain or shine, the women weave every day, and for one basic reason: money.

But all would agree that working, fulfilling their responsibilities to husbands and family, is the road to self-respect, social prestige, and ultimately praise in the eyes of God. "Working with wool,

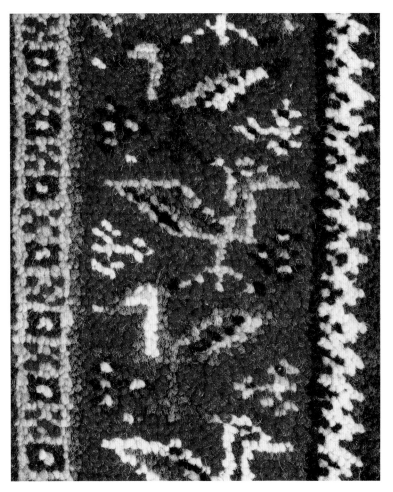

Left: Metdarin or meteedareen motif.
Right: The the thin yellow border at left shows the Izzalayn Anti Atlas rug motif of a "bead" or "jewel." The chicken motif, djej, appears in the center.

starting from the washing and dyeing, is a source of grace and blessings from God."

Traditional Designs

Weavers have a number of traditional designs to choose from. Three intricate designs can be traced to nature, everyday items, and vernacular architectural features. A diamond with little lines radiating from the edges is called *metdarin*, or *imizdareen*, or *meteedareen*, meaning "little feet" or "toes." This basic design, often used in borders, gives status to a carpet. Aicha Seqqat (page 54) says, "That design is like the foundation for a house"—that is, a basic element that must be included. Another popular design, "arches" (*bu laqwas*), is rectangular rather than rounded, resembling the local doorways. *Taboomrekte* is a diamond shape divided into quarters. "It's an ancient design that was used to decorate the tops of old adobe buildings."

The *taxalalt* design is based on the silver fibula or brooch used to fasten women's traditional clothing (Fadma Wadal wears this type of brooch in the photo on page 18). *Izzalayn*, "bead" or "jewel," appears as a small spot of color that serves as a highlight.

Then there is *djej*, the chicken. And what can be said of the star shape inside a hexagon, which is called *bimzghran* and means "ears"? It's safe to say that all these designs are descriptive of concrete rather than symbolic things, even though the comparison is not always easy to see.

Motifs of the Anti-Atlas and Middle Atlas Regions

Tafenzad: Middle Atlas rug design that looks like a line of bow ties, shown here at top and bottom, framing the menshar design in the center.

Hatif: Middle Atlas rug design of triangles composed of smaller triangles.

This whole design is called *lbelghra li kayrekebu lkhil* or "the shoes of men who ride horses." This refers to the fancy displays of riding where the horsemen's shoes are decorated with sequins. The red and orange diamonds inside the white-toothed menshar pattern are also called *l3ayun* or "eyes."

Menshar: Seen here in the center, it is a toothed zigzag Middle Atlas rug design called menshar, which means "saw." It is framed by *tafrawt*, or "flying birds," also a Middle Atlas rug design.

Taboomrekte: Ancient Anti-Atlas rug design of a diamond divided into quarters, also used in old adobe buildings.

Snan l3ajel: "Calf's teeth," a Middle Atlas rug design of small x's. Seen here in the rows between the vertically oriented tafenzad.

The top and bottom designs in blue are called **imighrz** or border. The widest zigzag with diamonds in it is called **menshar kbir, fih l3ayun** or "big saw with eyes in it."

These white diamonds are called **Hell-sedd** or "open-shut" because of how the design opens up to the full width, then closes to a point. This motif is also found in Khemisset rugs. Older women refer to the design as **3ynin lhejla** or "partridge's eye" in Arabic or **aleenen teskourt** in Tamazight.

Taxalalt: Anti-Atlas design based on the fibula or brooch used to fasten women's traditional clothing.

Variation of the little feet design.

Scenes of the Day in N'kob and Tazenakht

Clockwise from upper left:

Boy sitting at school wall in N'kob where local election results can be posted. The numbers represent political parties.

Rug sales at the weekly market in Tazenakht. Notice there are no women selling; a few were clustered near the wall in the background.

The stream running through N'kob provides water for irrigation.

Clockwise from upper left:
Girl in doorway in N'kob.

Ijja in N'kob with special local bread she made in oven to her right.

Boy at door of traditional granary or ighrem in N'kob, used for storing grain, documents, jewelry and to shelter women and children in times of tribal raids in the past. Many village homes were built using the same beautiful stonework.

Wool tools for sale at the open air market in Tazenakht: beaters on left, scissors to trim rug pile at top and cards at bottom.

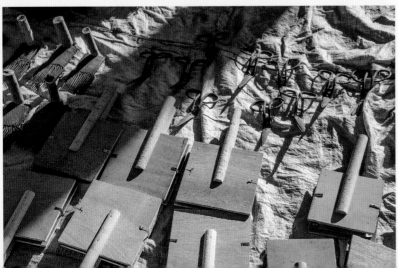

THE SEQQAT FAMILY

AICHA SEQQAT IS THE PRESIDENT of the Timnay Association of weavers in N'kob, an indication of her respected status in the village and the excellence of her weaving. She is also a midwife and one of two leaders chosen by the village women. The weaver's association meets at her home, and I stay there when I visit the village. My bed consists of a stack of her beautiful rugs on the floor. What could be more luxurious? I also like to stay with her because of her cheerful personality. It's hard for me to reap the full benefit of her humor and intelligence since she speaks only Berber, but her youngest daughter, Ijja, helps translate into Arabic.

I saw a clear example of her leadership at a meeting of the weavers several years ago. The income they earned from Internet sales was given to husbands, and depending on their inclinations, the men gave a portion directly to the women or more often spent it on household expenses. The family profited, but the women never received any cash for themselves. How to convince the men to give the women money? It was Aicha who spoke up, saying, "We could tell the men that if they'd give us a little something when we finish a rug, we might make the next one faster." Genius! Many women tried it, and it worked.

Now in her late sixties, Aicha was born and married in N'kob and raised four sons and three daughters. Until her husband died six years ago, he worked alongside her, shearing sheep, washing carpets, and trimming the pile on finished rugs. One of her sons preaches at a mosque, the youngest works as a waiter in Casablanca, and the son with whom she lives works in construction and farming, and buys and sells rugs part-time. Because there wasn't enough money to send her daughters to school, she says, "I taught them the craft so they could live on it." Ijja, the youngest, went to school for a year and learned Arabic while visiting family in the city of Agadir.

Aicha didn't learn to weave until she got married. "When I first came to my husband's house, there were no rugs. So I started to learn, and my carpets turned out nice. I got really good after the children were born. I sold them and bought things for myself and the children." As Aicha says, "A woman depends on weaving to live." It also influences how villagers see her. "They see her in a different way. The one who is better than others; they see her as useful, helpful for her husband and her home." Now that she is older, she cleans, cards, and spins wool for her daughter Ijja to weave, but rarely weaves herself.

In those earlier days, Aicha figured out what she needed for the house, either for furnishings or to buy food, and then set a sale price herself, taking into account the cost of wool and dye, the difficulty of the work, and her time. Sometimes she sold her rugs to a middleman who came to the house, and sometimes, when she was desperate for money, she sold the rugs to her son; she felt he would pay less. Occasionally she sold on the Internet or to tourists who paid rare visits to the village. In the past, she used the money for household expenses such as food and utilities. Now that her children are grown, she's able to afford some luxuries, such as tile for her kitchen walls. She and her daughter Ijja calculate that about half of their income now comes from weaving, and half is sent by the son working in Casablanca.

Aicha has woven several styles of rugs: the black and white chedwi, the "picture," the newer flatweave called terz, and women's

Aicha Seqqat, president of the Timnay Association of weavers, at her loom.

Ijja Id Ali Boufkir behind her loom.

traditional cream capes. "I liked to make a different kind each time, so if one style doesn't sell, the next one might."

I wanted to see what women value in rugs, so I asked Aicha which of those she liked best and why. She likes the chedwi because it's an old, traditional style. She also likes the women's cape. She says it is beautiful first because it shows her craft, then because it's large, and finally because of the intricate designs along the borders. It's interesting that for Aicha, tradition comes before design.

Aicha begins a new rug by choosing the colors. "I do use natural dyes sometimes, but it's difficult because it takes a long time. If you're using indigo, it takes two days to get ready. To make a good blue, you also need henna leaves, dates, and coal. Then you see what other colors will go with it." However, she doesn't plan the overall layout of the rug. Nor does she plan the designs she will use before she starts weaving. "When the loom is ready, you just start with whatever comes into your mind. It comes to your mind as you're weaving, little by little." This master weaver works from inspiration.

And what is life like for a young weaver in an isolated mountain village like N'kob? Busy, especially for **Ijja Id Ali Boufkir** when she and her mother, Aicha Seqqat, are hosting guests from abroad who are working on a book featuring her family. The fact is, she's always busy with chores and her weaving. Although only thirty-one, she is an expert, and part of a family of expert weavers.

Ijja lives in the family home with her mother, a married brother, and his family. She is not yet married, which used to be unusual for a rural woman over twenty, but is becoming increasingly common in a region where girls once married in their early teens. The oil crisis of 1973 changed all that. Young men could not find jobs and thus couldn't afford to marry. When they finally did find work, they often skipped over the women their own age and married younger singles. By 2014, improved educational opportunities for girls helped raise the average marriage age to twenty-five.

Ijja has completed first grade. Nowadays girls who are good students attend primary school in the village but seldom go beyond sixth grade, mainly because it means leaving home to live in a large town. Many Westerners think that girls should stay in school, but even if that were possible, it is not necessarily the best course for young women from isolated rural areas. For girls without a genuine drive for learning, staying at home and learning a craft that pays relatively well and produces beautiful things is preferable to suffering though ten more years of school hoping to get decent jobs, which are few and far between. To underline this critical condition, the Union of Unemployed University Graduates has been demonstrating in front of Parliament for years.

Even though Ijja has only a first-grade education, she is one of the few women in N'kob who speaks Arabic, which she learned while visiting her sister in Agadir. Ijja inherited her mother's sense of humor, and she instantly communicates her jokes to me in Arabic.

Ijja was about ten when she learned to weave from her oldest sister and her grandmother. She doesn't remember exactly how old she was when she knew she was good at weaving, but recalls it was around the time when King Mohammed VI visited the nearby town of Tazenakht to lay the cornerstone for a girls' dormitory. That occurred in 2003, when Ijja was about twenty, and the nationwide initiative to enable rural girls like Ijja to continue through high school was already in full swing.

Ijja's first fully accomplished weaving was a tarz, or two-sided weaving, which her grandmother taught her. Her grandmother also taught her how to make a wide variety of rugs and other textiles, and Ijja knows them all, including the older styles that are seldom made today. A rare traditional belt is among Ijja's favorite pieces. "It's like a book," she says. "When you forget something, you go back to read it." And also, the designs are pretty. The delicate designs are done in natural dyes harvested locally except for the indigo.

Ijja makes a rug when she gets an order for a particular design or when she needs one for her family home. Rugs are literally the furniture in N'kob; they are used for decoration and to sit on and sleep on. After finishing a rug, she waits about a week before beginning another. In the interim, she and her mother card and spin the necessary wool, which her brother buys in Tazenakht.

Like her mother, Ijja rarely starts a rug with an overall layout in mind. Instead, when something comes to her, she inserts the motif. After she's completed one or two motifs, she knows what the

third one will be. "It's like mirrors," she says. In other words, the design is symmetrical; once she's done half, she mirrors it in the other half of the rug. When asked if some of the designs she uses

Anaya Seqqat, Aicha's sister, has also been weaving since childhood.

have a meaning, Ijja laughed and said, "The meaning is that we make our living from them!" And she uses colors that she thinks will sell well.

A rug with the complex, two-sided flatweave called teereera.

Ijja's brother, a middleman, sets the prices for her rugs. Since he buys the materials for her, he knows the cost as well as the time she's spent weaving. When a middleman comes to buy her work, her brother does the negotiations. With the sale of her rugs, she is able to help support herself and her mother. Occasionally she buys something for herself, like shoes, rings, or cosmetic cream from the traveling merchant who comes to the village. Women rarely get out of town.

Ijja is at least the third generation of excellent weavers in a family known for producing exquisite rugs. Her mother's position as head of the village weaving association adds to the family's reputation for wisdom and skill. This fine mother-daughter pair ensures that the outstanding weaving of the area will continue to thrive.

Aicha's sister and Ijja's aunt, **Anaya Seqqat,** knows the design for the whole carpet when she starts weaving. "I never use a drawing on paper, not at all. I see the whole design in my mind." The sisters share the same bright laugh. Yet their approaches to weaving are very different. When Anaya describes herself as a weaver, she is careful to include all the steps involved in her craft. "My craft is that I get grass for my cows and sheep to eat, then I card and spin and dye the wool and weave and weave." Foraging for animal fodder is part of a woman's daily routine in the spring. Anaya puts that task ahead of weaving because she acknowledges how important animals are for her household and for her artisanry.

Anaya's husband farms their land and keeps a cow, a donkey, and a few sheep, which he grazes out in the barren hills. He is aging now and seldom works. Their two grown daughters learned to weave from Anaya.

Anaya has been weaving since childhood. "I just wove simple things, like the men's capes that come in one color." By the time she was twelve, she could do the complicated teereera design. She could also weave men's garments such as the *aznag* and *aheddoun,* as well as knotted and flatweave rugs.

As the main breadwinner for herself and her elderly husband, Anaya is fully involved in setting the price for her rugs. "It's all about our weaving, because my husband is old and worn out, and he can't earn much working in his gardens. I hurry to finish a rug and sell it so I can buy what I need for my house, like vegetables and meat, pans or dishes, and bottled propane gas." She includes the cost of her wool and dye in the price she sets, but not her time.

When she has to meet household expenses, she usually makes the more complex flatweaves called picture rugs. But Anaya has no preferences. "Everything I make with my own hands I like, that's for sure! Something I don't like, I wouldn't weave it in the first place!" But then she points one out. "I like the yellow one because of the color."

She uses plants and flowers for dye, but rarely. Mostly she buys commercial dye, though she can't always rely on the quality. "You buy and try it to see. Sometimes they say this is good quality, but when you use it, it's not that good. A good quality helps you with the colors, it gives you an exactly right color. With the other kind, you have to dye the wool two or three times to get a nice color."

At the age of sixty, Anaya is beginning to slow down and her eyes are not so good. Now she weaves with her daughter, and together they support the family. Her sister Aicha enjoys the same arrangement with her own daughter Ijja. Both young women are happy to be following in their mothers' footsteps.

A glaoui rug from N'kob, with flatweave (gray), pile, and twining (small bands of black and white). It has three borders, one mark of an excellent rug. The outer border has the meteedareen motif, Aicha's foundation of a good rug. Other motifs are chickens on the gray ground and taxalalt or brooches surrounding the blue center.

THE SOLITARY WEAVER OF TIZNIT

THE NIECE OF AICHA AND ANAYA SEQQAT has another story to tell. Fadma Buhassi was born in Amassine, a Berber mountain village just beyond N'kob, but married into N'kob, where I first met her. Whenever I came to photograph rugs for my website, Fadma Buhassi would happily spread the word. Fadma was a chosen leader of the village women as well as a midwife, reason enough for the women's confidence in her.

Five years ago, her husband got a job as a caretaker and guard at a rural school near Tiznit, and the family moved about 300 km south. The school was originally built as a jail by the ruler Moulay Ismail, but today its eighteenth-century adobe walls enclose gardens, olive trees, stables, and several buildings that provide the family with a beautiful place to live. Fadma's husband raises bees and cows and sells the milk to benefit the seventy students who attend classes there. After years of being a central figure in her village, Fadma has few neighbors. But she keeps busy milking the cows, preparing lunches for the students, and cooking and caring for her large family. She is also an excellent weaver.

At forty, Fadma has nine children. Two of her sons work for a company that searches for sources of water; the other two are still in school. Four of her five daughters dropped out after third grade and took up weaving. Fadma wishes they would continue their education and become more successful than her. It's rather poignant that a master weaver, mother of nine children, and leader of women doesn't

recognize her accomplishments, but today having a salaried job is valued more than achieving excellence at traditional work.

Fadma began weaving when she was five years old. She learned the basics from her mother, Rahma, a sister of Aicha and Anaya Seqqat. After some time, she started to weave on her own, and created designs on her own. The young girl had little choice: her father was out of work and she needed to help her mother support the family. By the time she was eighteen and blessed with her first daughter, she had become an expert weaver.

As we sipped tea in her large, sunny courtyard, Fadma's children spread out her rugs for display. There were pile rugs, flatweave rugs whose designs are based on traditional men's capes, and the flatweave rugs called "mountains" or "maps." These rugs are difficult to make because the patterns keep changing and are the same on both sides. In addition, Fadma makes traditional cream-colored women's capes, long men's bags, and smaller bags.

"I weave everything," Fadma says. "I make many kinds of things so I can sell more. But I like the pile rugs best. I can use them for furniture and also to keep my kids warm. When I have a guest or when someone special visits, I put out a red and blue rug that is my favorite."

Fadma uses many colors in her rugs. "Before I settle down to weave a rug or blanket, I decide on the colors. Then I wash, spin, and dye the raw wool. If I buy commercial yarn, I just dye it. There's a big difference between wool that I spin and yarn that I buy. With

Fadma in formal attire.

handspun wool, the carpet is very clean and very nice. I can sell it for a better price. A rug with handspun wool is prettier. After I do all that, I cut the yarn." (Some weavers cut the wool into short lengths for knots instead of using a long piece of yarn and cutting as they go.)

Like the other weavers, Fadma uses natural dyes only for small pieces. "If you need a little bit of dye, you can just gather a few flowers and plants and do it. But if you're making a large carpet, you need a lot of plants and flowers, and it takes a long time to gather them from the fields and woods, and to get them ready for dyeing. And you need to be sure it will come out a great color. If it's not the right color, you have to try again and again until you get the color you want. That's why it's very difficult to use natural dyes."

Although many merchants in Morocco will tell you that the rugs they sell are made with natural dyes, it's seldom true. A few old rugs used red from madder root, but on the whole, natural dye is rare. Considering the time and effort, it's easy to understand why.

"Like the colors, you have to think about the whole design from the first. When you start, you should know how it's going to end. Sometimes you might add some little symbols that come into your mind as you weave. You always keep thinking about the motif that's coming next, and you put in the perfect color for the next thing that you want to do.

"I've known some designs since I was small, but when I got really good at weaving, I started to weave motifs that I thought up myself. I don't look at any pictures; I just start weaving and thinking and make the motif." She pointed to the green geometric motif on a blue bag. "I did all of these motifs from what I imagined in my head."

Fadma also uses traditional designs. "Teereera is a popular style from long ago. It's important to keep something old in our life and in our weaving." Usually used in flatweaves and used by Fadma in knotted rugs as well, it's striking how varied this diamond design can be.

Since moving to this isolated school, Fadma weaves by herself. "The women here don't know how to weave. But in N'kob I wove with other women, and then with my daughters when they got old enough. Now I weave every month if I have an order, but if not, every other month. After I make bread and milk the cows, I can

Fadma Buhassi proudly shows her hennaed hands.

weave most of the day. When I have enough time, I can make six to eight rugs a year. When I have a lot of chores, I'm always thinking that I need to hurry up to have some free time for my carpet."

Carpets play an important economic role in Fadma's family, and she sets the prices on her own. "I look at the size, the design, the color, and if it's beautiful or not. I think about how hard the work was. I figure out the cost of the wool, the dye, and the wood used to heat the dye. I set a price so that if it's cut I'll still be happy. When you don't get enough money for all your materials, it's like you failed. If I really need the money, sometimes I still sell.

But if I don't get enough to cover my expenses and my time, I feel hurt. The work is very hard and you deserve to be paid for it. They shouldn't cheat you. It's beautiful to watch the rug as you weave, but if you start from preparing the wool, then dyeing, washing, spinning, and weaving, it's very hard."

Fadma's husband takes her rugs to Tazenakht and looks for buyers there. If he cannot get her sale price, he brings the rugs home. Fadma said she earned about $830 last year, and that, plus contributions from a working son, supported the family; her husband's company didn't pay him. She uses the money to buy food and clothing for the family, and if she has extra, she might take the children on a picnic.

Weaving has a value beyond its economic contribution. "If a woman is a really good weaver, people value her; she is really respected in her community." Fadma says, "Sometimes I worry about the future, but I don't think we'll ever give up weaving. Even when I have a lot of chores and housework, I still have time for weaving. We can't give it up. It's our craft, our calling."

Above: Fadma's husband and sons.
Right: Fadma milks one of the cows at the school where her husband works as a caretaker.
Opposite: A "maps" rug, one of many styles that Fadma weaves.

THE BLESSINGS OF COLOR AND WOOL

FATIMA ID RAHOU IS ONE of the younger weavers in the Timnay Development Association. She was born in the village of Tazoult and moved to N'kob after she married. She was thirty years old when she had her first child, a ripe old age for a woman in her culture. But Fatima is a bundle of energy and devoted to her craft.

She has to be dedicated because her husband, she says, does "almost nothing." Yes, he has a little land and a few sheep and cows and sometimes works a day or two in someone else's fields. His income is minimal, which is one reason that she wants her four small children to get good educations.

Fatima never went to school, not even the Quranic school in the area. These schools used to teach children to read and write and to memorize verses of the Quran. Today, the few remaining Quranic schools do that and also serve as preschools for children aged three to six. There is now a more modern preschool in N'kob, where one of the association weavers is the teacher. It costs one dollar a month per child.

Fatima learned to weave when she was very young. "I really wanted to learn the designs. I just watched my sister and my neighbors and asked them how they made the designs. When I was around fifteen or sixteen, I knew I was a really good weaver because I could make the designs myself, without my sister helping me.

"I like the flatweaves with squares because I can weave and sell them quickly. The pile rugs are more difficult to make, and it takes time to prepare the materials for them. But the pile rugs are really beautiful. I like to use the pile rugs for our children and for our home. They're part of my household collection, and if a friend or family or guests visit, I put out my best rugs for them. I only sell them if we really need money."

There's no vacation from weaving for Fatima because the family always needs the money. "I finish one rug and just start preparing for the next." If she has time to card and spin, she uses wool sheared from her own sheep. Otherwise she uses the spun yarn her husband buys at the souk. Rugs using her own wool bring a better price.

Her husband also buys her chemical dyes. She uses natural dyes when she weaves small articles that don't require much yarn. "If I saw a really beautiful belt and I wanted to do the same, I'd dye the wool in natural colors. But I wouldn't sell something I made with natural dye. If I used it for a bride's cape, I'd keep it for myself."

Fatima is drawn to lively colors, especially red and blue. Yet she is particularly proud of a long runner woven with handspun wool and dyed in bright gold, a color often used in N'kob and in southern Morocco in general. "Actually, I like all my carpets because I can use them for my house—and because they're mine."

Fatima creates as she weaves. "I don't know

Rug detail showing the iklan design. It's an older design that has become popular again recently. The black and white design on the sides is chedwi.

the overall design when I start, but I put motif after motif after motif. If I'm not in a hurry, I pay attention so my designs are very nice. If I'm in a hurry, I use *takhnift* designs, which look like embroidery." She often uses the *iklan* design, an older pattern that has recently become popular again and sells well. The black and white border is done with the twining technique called chedwi. "If I make a fancier design, I'll get a good price for the carpet. We use weaving to make a living. But my mother told me that when you're weaving wool, you receive blessings from God. And when you wash and spin and dye wool, you get more blessings from God."

Fatima's husband sets the prices and sells her rugs to middlemen in N'kob. Fatima has no idea about the costs of materials since her husband buys them for her. And she doesn't seem to keep track of her annual earnings. Her last rug sold for $85, but that was a few months ago. "Maybe my husband's income is more than mine," she concludes.

Fatima doesn't keep track of her time either. She estimates that one gold rug took her about five weeks to make. The small rug she's working on now has taken her three months, and she's still not done. "Weaving takes me a long time because I have young kids, and I have to feed them and bathe them and wash their clothes. And I also have to gather food for the cows." Given all her other duties, it's amazing that she produces as much as she does.

Fatima doesn't care if people say good things about her work. "I weave because I love to weave and I don't want myself or my children to be lacking anything. When there's weaving waiting for me and I don't have time, I get stressed and grumpy. But when I have time to weave, I can relax and I'm happy."

Fatima Id Rahou stands behind one of her rugs. Variations on this lattice design are common in the village of N'kob. It's called *dama* or squares; that's also the name for checkers.

ALL BUSINESS

FATIMA EL MENNOUNY IS AN EXPERT and prolific weaver as well as a productive mother. At age forty-four she just had her ninth child. Although she never went to school and cannot read or write, she is very savvy about rug quality and pricing. Her down-to-earth, direct manner, along with her outstanding weaving skills, have given her an extraordinary advantage in the marketplace. With her weaving income, she is building a new family home at the edge of the village.

Fatima's family is very dependent on the weaving trade. Her husband used to be a butcher but now sells sheep and carpets as a middleman. Two of her daughters are now old enough to produce rugs. She took them out of sixth grade so they could help support the family. None of her five girls has gone past primary school, but one of her boys went on to school in a nearby town. This is a common pattern in very rural areas; usually only boys continue their education outside the village, which means only they go past sixth grade.

Fatima learned to weave from her mother when she was twelve. She began with small rag rugs made from strips of old clothes. While many rag rugs in the United States are flatwoven, Moroccans often use strips of fabric to make pile. Because these rugs have little market value, most serious weavers don't make them. When they are made for the home, they often show great originality.

The same is true for "picture" rugs, which display a wide variety of innovative designs. Fatima prefers to make the picture rugs "mainly because we sell them for a lot of money."

Women's capes are also big sellers. A generation ago, the white capes were longer, and the colored decorations were done in real silk. Because silk is not available in most of Morocco, Fatima uses wool. Fatima also makes pile rugs, flatweaves with twining, and only sometimes the map rugs.

When Fatima is weaving a pile rug for her house, she uses whatever wool the family sheep provide. If she runs out, she buys raw wool that comes from nearby mountain villages and spins it. "But if I want to sell it, I just use yarn from the market." The rugs made of homespun wool have a sheen that commercially spun yarn does not. To dye the wool or yarn, she uses chemical dyes. "I buy expensive dye for market rugs because it gives me a beautiful color and I can sell it for a good price."

With enough children to help with the housework, cooking, and washing, Fatima is free to weave most of the day. "I weave from eight until the second breakfast, take a few minutes to eat, and weave until lunch. Then I go back to my weaving. If I don't weave, there is no money coming into the house."

Fatima considers a flatwoven picture rug her best work (see photo, page 68). True, it would probably sell for a lot of money, but she also thinks it's pretty because it contains teereera designs. "Also, I like it because I bought good-quality yarn and dye. If you don't get the best yarn and dye, you don't weave good carpets. If you pay a lot of money for dye, you get bright colors. You can tell if it's good or not when you're dyeing the yarn. If we use cheap dye, we waste our time, our water, and our firewood. Also, good yarn makes it easy to weave and bad-quality yarn gives you problems."

It took Fatima about six weeks to weave this rug, not counting the two weeks it took to prepare the yarn, washing and dyeing it. Preparing raw wool would have taken two or three months.

The rug measures "three by five," she says, but the rug is neither three meters nor three feet wide. Many weavers use their forearms for measuring length if a yardstick or tape measure isn't handy.

They estimate there are about two forearms to a meter, so the rug is about 1.5 x 2.5 meters, or 5 x 8 feet.

Sometimes rugs do not lie flat when taken off the loom. The teereera design is especially hard to weave flat. One solution is to wash the rug, stretch it using stakes in the ground, and then let it dry in the sun. "The sun also takes out bad colors. Sometimes they run, especially the natural yellow, and the sun will take that color away."

The colors she uses vary depending on whether they are for home use or for sale. "For the market, I choose any design and any colors. Sometimes a middleman gives me an order or a picture, and I do the colors and design he wants. But for my house, I choose black and blue. They don't get dirty so fast from the children, and you don't get all worn out cleaning the rug. Even after I've used those rugs a lot and they're old, they still sell for a lot of money."

Fatima knows the entire design of a rug before she begins weaving. "For my house, I know because I have to have enough yarn in the right colors for the whole design. For the middleman, I know in my head what the design will look like when I finish."

I wondered if the widely used and respected teereera design that filled Fatima's red rug had a meaning. "This design is important because we copied it from an old belt." When I asked if there was a more abstract meaning, such as a symbol of something like happiness or many children, Fatima said, "Yes, there is some relation to goodness, because the designs are old and very nice." Like most weavers I know, Fatima does not often see symbolism in the designs in her rugs.

"Then is weaving related to your religion?" I asked.

"I buy the wool from the market, wash it and dye it, then wash it again and weave it. From that I make some money that I use to buy tea, sugar, and barley for bread. This is the relation between religion and weaving: it fights hunger."

In line with her forceful personality, Fatima sets the price she wants for a rug. "If a middleman comes to my house and gives me the price I want, I sell it to him. If he won't give it, I wait for another middleman." She does not mention selling to her husband, a middleman, probably because she can get a better price from someone outside the family. She bases the price on the size of the carpet, the quality of the wool, and the complexity of the style. "I don't really count how much it costs for wool and dye. If I have some money,

Above: Fatima's flatwoven picture rug that she considers one of her best.
Opposite: Fatima sits on her picture rug.

I spend it on new materials for the next one; if I don't, I take the money from my savings." It's surprising that Fatima doesn't count the cost of her materials (but perhaps she knows them from the size). Nor does she mention her time.

One indication of Fatima's financial skill, though, is that she immediately knows how much she earns. During the last two months of spring, Fatima's rugs brought in about $850. In the win-

ter when she weaves full-time, she makes about $500 a month, the equivalent of a primary school teacher's beginning salary and an excellent income for a villager. "My income is more in rugs than my husband's is in business." Although Fatima's husband's business earnings fluctuate, her rugs always sell.

"If we have extra money, we save it for our house that we're building." That house, nearing completion, combines traditional stone with cement block, and it is at least twice the size of her current home. Besides being larger, the new house includes a roomy kitchen with built-in cabinets, and trim she's chosen in modern ceramic tile.

After the usual household expenses, she may buy shoes, scarves, or a "peignoir," a garment that Americans would call a bathrobe. During the chilly winter season when it sometimes snows, women wear them over their regular clothing. Peignoirs are unflattering, but they are warm. She also likes to joke, "I don't buy gold or silver because I have many kids. I just buy lots of soap and tea. When my kids grow up, I'll buy some gold for myself.

"People say about a good weaver that she's important. She earns good money so she can help her husband, her kids wear good clothes, and she helps to build a nice house. She isn't someone who's just sitting at home, whose kids look messy and don't have enough to eat. And sometimes she earns extra money to keep for herself."

One would think that a single young woman who is a good weaver might entice a man to marry her, but Fatima says no. "If she still lives with her family, maybe she can help them to repair an old house or buy furniture. But weaving has nothing to do with marriage."

As one of the best and most successful weavers in N'kob, Fatima relies on her usual business savvy to sum up the role of weaving in her village. "Weaving is everything for us. When we don't weave, we don't have anything. We get a headache if we don't sell a carpet. But if we sell our rugs, everything will be good and we will get money to meet our responsibilities for our children and our cows. If we don't sell our rugs, it's like closing the doors."

JAMILA SAMAA
THE ART OF WEAVING

JAMILA SAMAA CONSIDERS WEAVING AN ART, and she is the only weaver I talked with who spoke about creativity. Her superb weaving skills and intelligence underlie her grasp of the technical and economic aspects of weaving. In fact, her life has been shaped by her skills. Born and raised in N'kob, she never attended school and has never married. At forty-seven, she is the sole support of her aging parents and disabled brother. Having no husband and children to care for, she focuses on her work. Her job as a rug designer in her sister's workshop in Marrakesh has given her firsthand experience with "factory" production and has influenced her thinking about weaving as an artistic pursuit.

Since the age of fourteen, Jamila has been weaving all the styles native to her village: pile, flatwoven "picture" rugs, sometimes including the teereera design, and women's capes. Her work also includes the glaoui, which combines pile with twining and flatweave and is distinctive for containing the three weaving techniques.

In keeping with the growing interest in antique textile designs, she's revived a traditional pattern called *tahabant*. Although she has to card raw black and white wool together to create the gray background, "the color of the Sahara Desert," the rugs don't use much wool and the weaving is relatively fast. Knotted rugs take twice as much wool, are harder to make, and don't sell as well. Flatwoven rugs with the more intricate teereera design are also harder to make. "It's all done by counting the threads."

She insists that young weavers need an education

in order to count, to calculate how much wool is needed for a rug, and to understand money. Yet this master weaver has managed quite well without a day of formal schooling. Her rugs are beautifully made, and she knows every step that goes into them. Her hand-dyed colors are far more vibrant than the factory-made varieties available in the markets. She uses expensive chemical dyes, available at three shops in this small village. Once in a while, she uses natural dye in small amounts, such as spiny broom for yellow, walnut bark for brown, and madder for red. Experience is her teacher.

Before she begins a rug, she knows exactly how she will arrange the motifs she has in mind. But she doesn't choose colors she likes; rather she selects those she thinks will sell. The motifs have descriptive names, such as "little feet," but not symbolic meanings. However, she hints that sometimes they might, and she is cautious about using unusual patterns. "If you put something in a rug that has meaning in your life, you may not sell it," she says. "If you make a rug you'll use in your home, you might put in designs to remind you of something from the past." For her, the meanings of these designs are kept secret. And the influence of religion on weaving? "A rug has no relation to religion. It has a relation to making a living."

What is obvious immediately is that

Left: Detail of a glaoui style rug.
Opposite: Jamila Samaa stands in front of her home in N'kob.

Jamila's work is highly innovative. Her favorite rug is unlike any other made in N'kob (page 73). From a distance, the central design looks like a large red zigzag, but from close up it's a complex figure-ground pattern. The squares flanking it, filled with small motifs, are unusual too. A traditional aspect is the number of borders; the more elegant a rug, the more borders it will have.

"What was in my head, I put it in that rug, and I like it. You see, rugs are like art. Everyone puts what she has in her mind into her rugs. What I put in that rug, I did myself, not with someone else or a diagram. There's something in them that you don't find in other rugs. For me, that's art."

Jamila also has a clear sense of the economic aspects of weaving, including the economic injustices involved. The middleman who comes to her home to buy her work pays a good price, whether summer or winter. Yet she knows that the rug he buys from her will sell in the bazaars in Fes or Marrakesh for at least three times as much. She has done better by selling rugs through my project that posts them pro bono on the Internet.

Jamila's usual sale price is in line with the local market, plus the cost of her materials. "If I counted my time, I wouldn't even make a dollar a day." When she really needs money, she just sets a price that will sell the rug in a hurry. On average, she earns about $150 a month, which goes toward food and medicine. This is a decent amount for living in a village, but not enough for her to get her teeth fixed—something she would love to do.

When she worked in her sister's rug workshop near Marrakesh, she supervised the young women working there and furnished the designs for them to weave. "They were working in my head," she says. "If someone is working for you, they work fast just to get the money and they waste wool." The educated girls in the factory were mainly interested in dressing and living well and so were willing to do salaried work. They were paid by the square meter and earned $250 to $350 per rug, depending on the finished rug. This is much more than a village weaver makes, but the cost of living in the city is much higher as well.

Above: Jamila displays one of her pile rugs.
Opposite: Jamila's favorite rug.

At one time, Jamila dreamed of establishing her own workshop with women working for her. Certainly her dedication to excellence and her good business sense have given her a strong sense of self-worth, which is apparent in the way she carries herself and in the assurance with which she speaks. Yet a lack of capital and lack of interest among the local women have put that dream on hold.

For Jamila, being a good weaver is a way to independence. "She won't need anyone, she won't have to ask anyone for money, because she works for herself and depends on herself. And she has her freedom. But if you don't have money, you don't have anything to say." This echoes a popular Moroccan proverb: "If someone doesn't have money, his words are boring." In other words, "Money talks."

KEBIRA AGLAOU
WEAVING FOR THE GLOBAL VILLAGE

KEBIRA AGLAOU WEAVES THE FAMED RUGS of the Tazenakht region as well as completely original pieces. Her creativity runs deep and her reach is global. Recently she made three rugs based on photos of geometric designs created by a British artist and architect. Later the rugs were exhibited in Paris. Yet every week she attends the local rug market just to keep an eye on what's selling. Most women do not travel beyond their villages, much less deal with the larger world.

While the expansion of women's associations and cooperatives began a decade ago in other parts of Morocco, artisan development programs only burgeoned in the south in the past few years. Kebira is active in this new movement, representing the Timnay Association at conferences involving numerous craft organizations. Kebira never attended school, but because of her command of Arabic, her role as an officer and liaison with the Tinmay Association in N'kob has brought local textiles to the attention of the rest of Morocco. Ironically, they have been available to an international audience since 2001, when they appeared on my website (www.marrakeshexpress.org). She rose to this position partly because she is younger than many of the women in the group, including the current president, Aicha Seqqat, partly because she lives in town rather than in N'kob so she can travel easily, and in no small way because of her outgoing and determined personality. Her relationship with her husband Ahmed is unusually

Some of the varied designs in a map rug.

egalitarian, and his knowledge of the Internet has been essential for filling orders from abroad. And thanks to his encouragement and my support with the paperwork, in 2016 she participated in the International Folk Art Market in Santa Fe, New Mexico, a juried exhibit of worldwide crafts. On our way to obtain her visa in Casablanca, she told me it was her first trip on a train. Many new experiences awaited her, experiences that would benefit her and the other members of her weaving group.

Kebira was born in the village of Azzki, across the snowcapped High Atlas Mountains from Marrakesh. After she married Ahmed, she moved to the dusty market town of Tazenakht and became the mother of two sons and a daughter who are as bright and as curious as their parents. At the age of forty, Kebira enrolled in one of the many literacy programs designed for adult women. She's learned her letters and can now sign her name. Her well-educated husband is employed as an administrator at a cobalt factory outside town.

Kebira began weaving when she was eight, helping her mother make a pile rug with an abstract pattern in black and white. "I just watched what my mother did and followed her, that's all. It was easy for me. By the time I was fifteen, I could tell the difference between a good rug and a bad one. All rugs are pretty, but I like knotted rugs a lot better than those 'map' rugs. I'll make them, but I can't bear to furnish with them. When you spread them out, they look like machine-made wall-to-wall carpet. Besides, they're difficult to weave. With knotted rugs, you just work along, but with the map

Kebira Aglaou has a tremendous knowledge of weaving, specializing in three specific styles, and is able to innovate.

rugs, the designs change. Each triangle is separate, and they have to be the same on both sides."

Despite her objections, Kebira produces the map rugs in gold, along with every type of rug, cape, and bedspread unique to this area. "My mind is full," she says. "I really know a lot of things."

One indication of her "full mind" is something I have not seen anywhere else in Morocco: a woven picture of the mountains near her home. The small rug is prominently displayed on her wall, something else I rarely see. Actually, I have seen picture rugs of Berber brides or horsemen, but they are tawdry and usually made in government-sponsored tourist shops, nothing as authentic and lovely as Kebira's weaving, which captures the changing colors of the mountains in early evening.

Kebira has re-created an antique belt handed down in her family. Women used to wear them over loosely wrapped dresses, but now they are set aside as family keepsakes or sold to collectors, often foreign.

Although Kebira says she's always weaving, she slows down during Ramadan as well as the hot summer months. Normally she works in a room just off the open roof of her house, and though

Left to Right: Details of women's cape or bedspread with sequins, crocheted doily, and randa trim on a jellaba sleeve.

the sun makes it hot, it's far from the noise of her family. She weaves alone, but before she married she wove with her sisters and her mother. She sounds wistful as she recalls those early days.

Kebira's hands are seldom idle. She knits, crochets, makes needle-woven trim for women's jellabas, makes macramé baskets, and does Fes and cross-stitch embroidery. "You really need good eyes," she admits. But these popular crafts have a long tradition in Morocco, and as we shall see, needlework offers thousands of young women a creative outlet as well as extra income.

Most often, Kebira works on rugs. "You know why? I can earn more. If I see this kind sells well and at a good price, I make it. If I see another, I make that. I follow the market. And I don't make a rug until I know where that money will go. For example, if I want to buy something, I put that price on the rug and I sell it. If it's not enough, I'll weave another rug to make up the amount I still need."

Depending on the colors she plans to use, she buys either raw wool or spun yarn, which she dyes herself in order to achieve the lovely rich colors for which her region is noted. "People really prefer to get white yarn and dye it, because the dye used for yarn at the souk isn't like that you use at home. It's *not* the same." If she decides on golden yellow, her relatives in N'kob gather prickly broom for her in the mountains. "Raw wool takes on the colors better. When you wash the wool, it shines and looks like new. But my grandmother told me that it's bad to wash raw wool with detergent because if you scrub too hard, the natural oil will come out." Unfortunately, detergent is widely used today, and much yarn looks dull.

The cost of wool and dye goes into Kebira's sale price. She also counts her time, "not by hours but by days, weeks, or months." Independent woman that she is, Kebira then takes her rugs to the special women's rug market, held on Wednesday afternoons in Tazenakht. There she waits until some middleman buys and carries them off to Marrakesh to sell.

How much do the middlemen and shop owners mark up the price of rugs? Kebira and Ahmed took a trip to Marrakesh to find out! "I went with my husband to different shops. The rug they buy here for $200 sells for $600 in Marrakesh. That's triple the price."

Ahmed carefully explains why the shop price is so expensive. "They buy from women who are needy and have to support their kids. 'I pay her on the spot,' the shop owner tells you, 'but after I buy, I have to eat and drink and to wait for a buyer.' He admits he sells it for a high price."

It works the same way in the provincial town of Tazenakht. The big middleman tells the little middleman to buy a rug he likes and not to go over a certain price. If that price is $50, the junior middleman may start offering a woman $40. If he buys it, the big middleman may give him anywhere from two to five dollars, because he didn't have to travel far to buy and deliver the rug. Then the big middleman takes the rug to a daily auction in Marrakesh or Fes. But Ahmed says it's hard to know how much the big middleman earns. His sister's husband is a middleman, but he won't tell.

A merchant's profit may be a secret, but a weaver's income is often a mystery. Kebira can't say how much she earned last year, but in the last two months, she made $520. She doesn't know how many rugs she makes a year either. "My husband earns a lot of money, me just a little. A rug isn't like a job. Every month he's paid his salary, and me, I could sell several rugs in a month or I could sell nothing at all." She guesses that her income is around 10 percent of his.

"Ahmed pays for food and the children's clothing. I may buy dishes for the house and clothes for myself. And one big thing: I helped my husband buy an apartment in Marrakesh. Now I hope to sell more rugs for items we need. So far, I bought furniture for the children's bedroom. We're going to replace the windows and then furnish the whole apartment, God willing."

A knotted rug of Kebira's with central medallions.

THE AMASSINE STYLE

AMID THE BROWN FOOTHILLS leading toward the snowcapped Anti-Atlas Mountains, the houses of Amassine are practically invisible. Although this remote village lies only forty miles from N'kob, there is no direct route between them. Even the new paved road makes the trip arduous, leaving these two extraordinary weaving centers as isolated from each other today as they were in the past. Cut off by mountainous terrain, it is no wonder that the weavers of Amassine create unique rugs, which, for the intrepid, make the journey worthwhile.

Weavers in this timeless place experience few encroachments from the outside world. There are no televisions or satellite dishes crowning the flat adobe roofs. On the hill above the village stands a fortified granary built centuries ago to safeguard the wheat, precious valuables, and sometimes women and children from lawless marauders. Although seldom used today, every family maintains a small storage space protected by a low door and key.

On the brown plain below, the walled Jewish cemetery is an emotional reminder of the social upheaval of the 1960s when one-third of the village population departed for Israel. They were not expelled from the village, but encouraged by Israel to emigrate. Hamid Idali Haddou remembers that when he was growing up Jews and Muslims shared holidays and family celebrations. "Buses came to take them

Opposite: Amassine.
Right: Rqia Ait Taleb and her devoted son Hamid.

away. It took the buses three days to get here from the main road because they kept breaking down. Everyone cried when the Jews left, them and us."

Hamid introduced me to this village and his extended family. He is the devoted son of **Rqia Ait Taleb,** the respected matriarch of three generations of weavers. The bonds are thick. Rqia is the mother-in-law of **Aicha Al Borbouch** and the sister-in-law of **Fdila Azreg.** Fdila's husband is the uncle of Aicha's husband. The women are related by marriage and by their craft. Although Rqia is blind, she still spins. And she still wears the intricate traditional belt once common in this region, the only woman I have ever seen do so.

Aicha, a shy woman of fifty-two, is the mother of two teenage daughters, the younger girl in her last year of primary school. Her nineteen-year-old daughter is already a weaver who works on rugs with friends and also with her mother. Aicha's husband is a farmer who grows corn, apples, onions, barley, and saffron, the major cash crop in this area. In autumn, Aicha and the girls gather the crocus flowers that produce this costly spice, pick out the red stigmas by hand, and dry them. Her husband handles the sales.

Aicha's aunt, Fdila, is an outgoing woman in her sixties who has raised five sons and two daughters, cooks, cleans, and takes care of the sheep, and still has time to weave. Born in the mountain village of Tajoujchte, she married and moved to Amassine as an adolescent bride. Her husband, who died two years ago, owned the general store, which supplied

Fdila Azreg weaving at her loom.

Aicha and Fdila produce different styles of rugs. Aicha makes only knotted rugs, claiming she doesn't know how to make the chedwis, which include a twining technique, in which pairs of weft threads are twisted around the warp threads to create a pattern. Fdila, on the other hand, specialized in large carpets combining flatweave with colored geometric designs and twining done in black and white or colored geometric designs. (These designs are called *tihuna* in Amassine and teereera in N'kob, although twining is chedwi in both places.) She also made large pile rugs. In recent years, Fdila has become less ambitious, weaving small rugs that are either knotted, done in flatweave, or a combination of the two. "I like all the styles and did them all," Fdila says, "but I can't do them now because I'm tired."

The women tend to judge their rugs by how hard or easy they are to make. Function is also important. The rugs that Aicha keeps in her home display the fine craftsmanship of her mother-in-law Rqia. Of these, she prizes an unusually dark rug. "It's very old, and when I'm dead they will wrap me in it and take me to the cemetery. It's our custom." As she and Fdila are quick to point out, the rug is not buried with the body. People are buried in shrouds, not coffins, and after the funeral the family takes the rug home. In Amassine and N'kob these black and white flatweaves are called *leHemel* ("to carry" in Arabic), perhaps because they are used to carry people to their graves.

Rugs serve many practical purposes, and the primary motivation for making them is also practical: money. As Fdila puts it, "I do it for sugar," even though her son and his family care for all her needs. The rug she is currently working on will take three or four months to make, for which she may earn $20. She might take off a month before starting another. However, during her "free time" she will be preparing the wool for her next rug.

Aicha is fortunate because her husband helps people shear their sheep and is paid in cash and in wool. Otherwise she and Fdila buy yarn and chemical dyes at the local shop. Neither woman knows how to use natural plant dyes, but they certainly know how to clean, comb, card, and spin wool.

These days Aicha assists her daughter at the loom. The tables have turned, and now her daughter even chooses the designs. Before her daughter took charge, Aicha wove "whatever came to

household necessities as well as spun wool and chemical dyes.

Both women began to weave when they were five years old. "Look at my hands and you can see how long I've been weaving," Fdila says. "See the marks from the wool beater? I've done lots of hard work. I've ground corn and wheat by hand and used an adze to chop firewood. And after all of that," she laughs, "I'm still not really good at weaving."

mind and whatever colors I wanted. But the designs I started with would always be at the other end of the carpet as well. As for the colors, I like black, red, green, yellow, and maroon."

Since Fdila's daughters left the house, she has been working on her small rugs alone. Naturally she chooses her own designs, and from the moment she starts to weave she knows the overall pattern of the rug. When I asked her how she comes up with the designs, Fdila shot back, "How did you decide to come to this village?"

"It's my job," I replied.

"It's the same for me," she said.

After the women complete the rugs, the men in the family handle the pricing and sales. Aicha's husband doesn't ask her how much time she puts into a rug but does keep track of the wool, yarn, and dye he purchases. "A middleman comes to the house, and we fight about the price until finally we settle." Aicha's husband does the actual bargaining, then tells her the final sale price for each rug, and she seems happy with that.

Fdila's son drives his public transportation van to Tazenakht and sells her rugs at a shop or at the men's outdoor market on Thursday mornings. She's not always pleased with the price he gets, but she has no choice. "My son buys food, pays for electricity and water, buys my clothes, my weaving materials—everything." Neither woman receives any cash for her labors, but since the money goes toward the general support of their families, both consider it a fair arrangement.

Surprisingly, there is a third, nontraditional way for weavers to earn money in this conservative village. A European company commissions women to weave custom designs using natural dyes. Since sheep in this area produce excellent wool, some village women are hired to clean, card, and spin it. Then a Moroccan employee who is a specialist in making natural dyes provides the weavers with the colored yarn along with a picture of a rug design for them to follow. Women are just paid for their labor.

Fdila and her two daughters weave for the company even though those rugs take longer to weave and are made differently. "The technique is the same as ours, but he uses one row of knots and two rows of weft, and we use four. The colors are complicated, and he uses thinner yarn, so it takes a long time. The company rugs also use different designs. They look like pictures more than our

designs. The weavers just copy a photograph. It's hard and takes a long time, but if you're smart, you can do it."

The special skill and extra time required deter some village women from weaving for the European company. Aicha and her daughter only make knotted rugs for the local market. Although Fdila is willing, the work is sometimes frustrating. If the design isn't done perfectly, she has to start over again.

"We prefer our local designs because they're ours and it's easy for us, and the European man's are difficult. But it's good in the

Aicha Al Borbouch carding wool.

end, because you earn a lot of money if you weave a carpet for him."

According to Aicha and Fdila, a small rug sold locally brings in about $13, and about $16 if made for the company. The differ-

Rqia, like many older women, stopped weaving when she couldn't see very well but continues to clean, card, and spin wool. She wears an intricate traditional handwoven belt.

ence seems slight, but as they reminded me, the company supplies the raw materials, and though the rugs take longer to make, the women don't have to spend time washing, carding, spinning, and dyeing the wool.

Many weavers would like work that promises regular orders and a dependable income. But a possible danger is that local styles and creativity may fade. At present, women in the village are choosing whether to stick with their traditional designs or to try the new international product. Fdila does both.

Weaving represents a minor part of each family's income. Aicha earned $50 for a small carpet that took two weeks to make, and she usually weaves one a month. The bulk of the family income comes from the sale of apples and saffron on their farm. Fdila earned $20 for a small rug that took her four months to weave, mainly because her eyesight is failing and she can't work any faster. Fortunately, her son makes a good living transporting people in his van. For both women, the men of the family provide a decent income.

The presence of a European company that directs and buys the women's wool and weaving skills provides a glimpse into the future, one that many less-isolated villages lack. Although a few women elsewhere are getting orders for unusual rugs from abroad, the views of Amassine women about participation in this new kind of weaving allow us to see what this change looks like from their perspective. Although the women's financial contributions to the family are minimal, weaving is vital to their self-esteem and social standing. People comment on women's weaving skills, and at the time of marriage, weaving helps. People will say, "She's good at weaving; that's why she got a husband." However, the possibility of increased income, along with the introduction of European designs, has been met with caution.

"Weaving is what gives meaning to our lives," says Aicha, who doesn't weave in the new style even for money. "I wake up and pray that God may be with me as I'm weaving."

Fdila agrees. "When you are weaving, you enjoy it and are optimistic because you have a goal you're working for." She hopes that God will count her work as good deeds and forgive her because she didn't take care of her health and wore herself out by weaving. "It's a good way to earn an income, and it's a good way to see the face of God in heaven."

A MODERN WOMAN INNOVATES

HABIBA LRHACHI IS A CITY GIRL who lives in Tangier. But she grew up on a small farm just outside the village of Ben Smim, in the Middle Atlas Mountains, amid hills covered with daisies and wild lavender. Like her mother, Fatima Fidl (page 22) and her sister, Fatima Lrhachi (page 28), she loves to weave. The main difference is that Habiba stayed in school and went on to university. Education put her on a different trajectory, in some ways a more difficult one, but an increasingly common path as more young women continue their schooling.

I met Habiba in the fall of 2002 when I was expanding my online marketing project for handwoven rugs. She and a Peace Corps volunteer had brought rugs from her village to sell at a craft fair at Al Akhawayn University where I was teaching that year. When she heard about my project, Habiba was eager to get involved. She was desperate for a job. She had been teaching literacy for a local nonprofit organization, but the director had absconded with the funds and had not paid the instructors. Since then, she had been looking hard and long for a position commensurate with her skills. Her problem was all too common among educated young women, especially in the rural area where she lived.

Immediately Habiba became my assistant, helping me photograph, measure, and weigh rugs and eventually doing the photography and written descriptions of the rugs and the artisans. She was well on her way to becoming a full partner when economics intervened. Her salary was based on a percentage of the rug sales, and Habiba needed to earn more. She ended up working at an assembly plant in Tangier.

Later, when she got tired of standing on an assembly line for eight hours a day, she worked as my research assistant, surveying

Habiba knits in her apartment in Tangier.

people impacted by a new harbor project on Morocco's beautiful Mediterranean coast. She was excellent! Her university degree in cultural geography was a boon, and she enjoyed helping me formulate questions, conduct interviews, and record data. Not infrequently, she suggested better ways of accomplishing a task. But that was a short-term grant. Currently Habiba is head of housekeeping in a Tangier hotel, a job for which she earns a decent salary but for which she is grossly overqualified. At the age of forty, she was recently married.

Weaving is the unifying thread in Habiba's life. "When I was a child, I used to watch the women who made rugs. With my eyes, I tried to 'steal' what they were doing. My family didn't want to teach me how to weave. They didn't think I'd profit from it. They wanted me to open up, to go to school and study.

One of Habiba's pile rugs.

"We had an old neighbor lady who worked wool and sang as she wove. I tried to work wool and sing those songs, just like her. Everyone laughed at me, singing the songs of an old woman. Even though my sister laughed at me, she gave me a special present, a small loom made out of sticks. I practiced on it. But one day I disobeyed her, and she broke the loom. It didn't stop me. I still had the desire to learn everything I saw: knitting, crochet, macramé, and henna tattooing. I used to 'steal' those skills, a little here, a little there, from older women. I'd just watch, the ideas would percolate, and then I'd try to do them."

As she grew up, Habiba learned Fes embroidery and knit stylish sweaters for her nephews and nieces. She also made hats, gloves,

shawls, and socks, all with no instruction. Her elaborate henna designs were good enough to decorate the hands and feet of several family brides.

She also excelled in school. Eventually she went off to the university in Meknes, about an hour away, a big step for a rural girl. The family had pinned their hopes on her younger brother, but perhaps he was needed to help his father on the farm. It was Habiba who completed university and who now sends money home to the family. (Her brother lives at home with them and contributes money, too.)

After graduating, she returned to the farm and took up henna, embroidery, and crochet again and added macramé, which she proudly noted was an international craft. Although her mother had a working loom at home, Habiba did not take up weaving until she started helping me market rugs from Ben Smim on the Internet.

"My love for rugs returned. Working with my neighbors, I learned to judge good work and attractive colors. In 2003, I decided to make my first rug. My brother's wife and my mother helped me prepare the wool and showed me what to do." Habiba calls it a "bio" rug—the term used for organic produce—because it was made with natural white and black wool. "When I started that rug I didn't really know how to weave. The design had mistakes in it and it was loosely made. It was ugly. But by the time I got to the other end, it was pretty. And even though it was uneven, it sold."

For her next effort, she decided to work from a picture. Although weavers employed in workshops and factories use drawings, traditional weavers do not. It was a beautiful rug with a flower design in the center and around the edges. It sold at the International Folk Art Market in Santa Fe, though later she regretted having parted with it. By then she had become a good weaver and knew how to do all the designs and how to correct errors on her own.

With the leftover wool, she made a small, child-size rug with a diamond design in colors. She sold that rug when tourists visited her home. She makes pile rugs, but doesn't know how to weave the more complex flatweave designs.

Three years later, Habiba moved to Tangier in hopes of finding a job. The city is a tax-free industrial zone that attracts European clothing companies and automobile assembly plants. Young women usually find employment in sewing factories. Habiba landed a job in an auto factory, assembling wiring for cars. Her subsequent work with me on the harbor project, involving topics she had studied in school, is probably as close as Habiba will come to using her education fully. "I'll never forget it," she says. "I loved that period."

Next she chose hotel work because she enjoyed dealing with tourists, so much so that at one point she considered opening the family home as a bed-and-breakfast. Realizing the difficulties, she accepted a secure job with steady pay as supervisor of the hotel's housekeeping staff. Like many single women, before marriage she rented a small apartment with a female cousin. In the summer, she accommodated family guests, who love to visit Tangier and the beach.

Habiba's small apartment inspired her to make a new style of rug (opposite). Instead of a big loom, she used a crochet hook. She bought the wool already spun and dyed and spent three months working on it at night while watching television. "I did a modern design, not our old designs, and I tried new colors. I thought, 'Machines make rugs and wall-to-wall carpet with those modern designs, so why don't weavers start using those contemporary styles?' They need to develop new ideas in order to market their products. Thank God the traditional styles exist, because we rely on them. But the modern ones add a new flavor."

She used a new method for this different style of rug, which is one of her favorites. "I like to create a design in my head, and I succeeded in carrying it out with my own hands. For this, I used paper and pen and drew what I wanted to make." Habiba's drawing not only contains the design; it also includes dots to follow for placing the knots.

Habiba is one of the few weavers I know who is willing to innovate. In fact, her new rug is a by-product of current social trends. Growing numbers of working women with limited time to weave and limited space for a loom are being exposed to new ideas that may change the direction of Moroccan weaving.

Many Moroccan women weave constantly, either because they need the money or a new carpet for their home. Habiba weaves "only for love, to make something with my own hands." She weaves at night and on weekends. Like many Americans, she weaves when she's stressed. "Weaving makes me forget my problems and my tiredness."

Most of the rugs she's made have sold to foreign buyers. To set the prices, she just picked a number, without calculating her time, materials, or profit. She used the money to install indoor plumbing, a toilet, and a shower in her family home, additions that have made a huge difference in their lives.

"Our Islam tells us that work is worship. People were created to work, to provide something beautiful or good. Our Islam always tells us to be productive, either to benefit yourself or to help people and society."

Habiba says that you can measure a woman's intelligence by whether she knows how to make something. To be *hadga*, "skillful," you must be smart to begin with, be a good cook and skilled artisan, and be able to solve problems. Interestingly, rural people rarely use the word *dekka*, "intelligent," but instead use *hadga* to praise accomplished women.

Habiba says that in her region weaving has lost its value as a vital skill. But unlike her mother, Fatima Fdil, she's optimistic about the future. The revival is partly due to the nonprofit organizations that are giving women looms and weaving tools. And then there's the expanding market created by the Internet.

"I had the idea of selling on the Internet the moment the Internet began. I knew it opened up the world, and the first idea that came to me was to promote rugs from our region. I had no idea how it worked, how you get online. But I stopped thinking about further education, about getting a visa to go abroad. I just knew the Internet was a way to connect with the outside world.

"And then I met Susan [the author of this book] at a rug exhibition at Al Akhawayn University. The moment she gave me a business card and said, 'I sell rugs on the Internet,' she touched me. I had the idea, but I didn't have the key to enter. So thanks to her I learned how to profit from the Internet, how to help my country, how to do something that I'm proud of.

"When I knock on a woman's door and give her an envelope with payment for a rug that she used to just wipe her feet on, that she was going to throw away or burn, or was hidden away, gathering dust, well, one day I bring her an envelope that she uses to help her children or solve a crisis or escape from a debt. That little effort I made always makes me proud."

AN ACTIVIST IN AIT HAMZA

Kenza Oulaghda is a traditional Berber woman and a multitasking cyber-merchant never without her two cell phones. Equipped with a high school education, a thirst for helping local people, and knowledge of the workings of non-profit development organizations, she is breaking new ground for the rug weavers of Ait Hamza.

Her small adobe village lies on a green plain at the northern edge of the Middle Atlas Mountains. Some schoolchildren, especially in Quranic schools, still write their lessons on wooden boards, using a mixture of wood ashes and soot for ink. Yet the 6000 villagers, living only sixty miles from Fes, enjoy the modern conveniences of electricity and smartphones.

Kenza is forty years old, single, and the guiding light of the Tithrite Association for Development. She didn't learn to weave until she left high school at the age of nineteen; girls in school don't have time to weave, and that is a threat to the craft. For years, her mother prodded her to take up the loom, but Kenza didn't see the point of it. But as she matured she realized that the income her mother earned from weaving contributed to the well-being of the family.

In fact, Kenza had two mothers. When her father's first wife couldn't have children, he married again. They all lived contentedly in

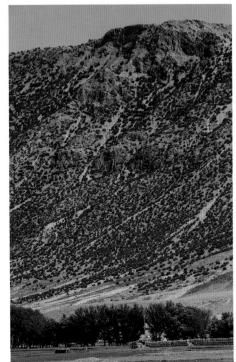

one house, and both women raised the children. Even though the family didn't have much money, her father and mothers gave her whatever she needed for her education. It was a hardship because, like most rural girls, she had to attend a boarding school in a larger town for junior and senior high. While her father paid for school supplies, her mother provided spending money for food, clothes, and extras. "I was lucky I had two mothers," Kenza says. "Mothers always do more for their children."

During summer vacations, Kenza helped her mothers with their knotted rugs. "Those rugs need a lot of hands. The more people, the faster it goes." Kenza can make a pile rug on her own but hasn't mastered the more complex flatweaves. As she admits, "I'll never be a specialist, like the women who started at age seven."

Kenza recently learned how to weave on a floor loom. Though floor looms are traditionally the province of men, an organization donated them to her group, and she finds the work easier. "With the floor loom, you just beat a row once, but with rugs, you have to pound all along the row with the beater. With a pile rug or a flatweave, you can't make any mistakes, and the work is hard on your shoulders." Still, the traditional rugs are what sell and what they make.

Flatweaves are the best known and best made rugs of the Middle Atlas region. They vary from alternating plain and patterned horizontal stripes to an overall design. For home use, women weave simple blankets in natural ivory wool with a stripe or two. Yet from a young age they are expected to produce

Opposite: One of Kenza's favorite rugs; the design was inspired by a nomadic shepherd.
Right: The village of Ait Hamza, Kenza's home town, is about sixty miles south of Fes.

Above: Kenza models an exquisite wedding cape.
Above right: Older women show Kenza how to wrap the *lizar* to be worn under the cape.
Below right: Kenza shows the the intricate design on the inside of the wedding cape.

a wide variety of styles.

"People used to say that a girl who didn't know how to weave was crazy. When she marries and goes to live with the groom's family, the bride has to take her wedding cape, a flatweave rug, a knotted rug, and a mat made of palmetto grass woven with colored wool.

"Mats made of palmetto grass are seldom woven anymore be-cause there isn't much grass around and it takes a long time. Wom-en have to soak the palmetto grass in the irrigation ditch or river for fifteen days so it gets soft. Then they pound it with a rock and drop it in boiling water until it gets softer. Even so, the women's hands get rough and raw." Though harder to work than wool, the mats are far more practical than modern plastic ones: the palmetto grass is left long on the back of the rugs and provides insulation from the cold floor in winter.

Of the necessary items in a bride's trousseau, the most presti-gious is the wedding cape, which the bride first wears sequined side out for the henna ceremony. (This explains the rust-red spots often found on older capes.) Modern brides wear *qaftans* or *tqashet* under their sequined capes, but in the past, they simply wore a long cloth, the *lizar,* wound around the body. That custom has disappeared so completely that Kenza needed the older women to show her how to wrap it. Brides also covered their faces with a colorful satin scarf, their version of a wedding veil. And girls used to marry very young, at twelve or fourteen. Now they may not marry until they are thirty-five or forty, or not at all.

Weaving items for sale requires a substantial investment in raw materials. Members of the Tithrite Association either use wool from their own sheep or buy it at the market. The local *Timahdite* breed supplies good, long-staple wool, which, Kenza says, was even better when the sheep ate grass and herbs in the wild. Sometimes the women buy wool carded and spun by machine in order to save time, a factor that affects pricing. "If we work all the wool by hand, we'd have to ask $5 more per square meter just for the labor." Using the machine-spun wool, the group produces knotted rugs in the Beni-Ouarain style, which is composed of black geometric designs floating on a white background. These rugs were originally made by the Beni Ouarain tribe in northeastern Morocco, east of Fes. The wool was loosely spun and quite thick, so the rugs looked a lot like a real sheepskin. The best older ones have a silky sheen. They have become popular in modern western homes, both for the often "free-form" designs and for the neutral colors.

"But the wedding cape and men's robes and capes require special wool and a special technique that calls for cards as well as combs. Each woman in our association specializes in a particular task. For the cards, the wool needs to be white and clean and have long threads. After the wool is carded, the women set it aside for a while, sort of like letting yeast in bread rise, so it won't break. The warp threads need to be fine and strong, and that's done by combing the wool until it's as soft as silk. Older women know how to do that. Then the spinning. The spindles are like the little ones used for producing jellaba buttons. They draft and stretch the wool until the yarn is very thin. There are many steps for making these garments, and each one is difficult.

"The work is amazing considering that most of the women in our group started out by making simple flatweave rag rugs, because wool was expensive. But when they switched to wool rugs,

they applied the same method to the rag rugs and began knotting them too." Whether the rugs imitate traditional patterns or contain totally new designs, they display a remarkable advance in technical ingenuity. The new designs illustrate the creativity one often finds in rugs for the home rather than for the market.

Another change has been the shift from natural to commercial dyes. Although henna leaves and pomegranate rinds are plentiful, madder root, used for red, is now hard to find in the nearby woods. Weavers also dyed with a plant called *dbagh*, used by tanners, which created a pale mauve. This rare color, called "pigeon's neck," was found only in this area and has disappeared from the contemporary weaver's palette.

The size of rugs has also changed. Flatweaves made for sale are often smaller than the long narrow ones, about five x eight feet, once made specifically to fit rooms in villagers' homes.

Although some things change, Kenza also respects tradition. One rug that Kenza made and especially admires was made in

Heavy beater to beat the wool.

the old style but with an individual stamp (see page 86). She was inspired by a nomadic sheepherder who never went to school but earned enough to raise his children and see them married. Famed for his rug designs, he told Kenza, "I sleep and I dream, and in the morning I make the design. That's how my revelation comes." Yet according to Kenza, his designs are steeped in Berber tradition. "For example, the designs along the edge were once used to decorate women's slippers. If we went to other villages, we'd also see them in silver jewelry and in belts. This rug contains a symbol of power in the black as well as the bright colors of sun, sky, and light."

Certain practices shuttle back and forth between old and new ways of doing things. "When I learned to weave with my mother, we didn't have a special layout in mind. We didn't say, 'We're going to do this or that rug.' Perhaps we'd borrow a rug from that man who dreams designs and take parts from it. We'd just measure where the center was and work towards it. Since we knew the designs, we'd just let our ideas run free. But after we attended training workshops last year, I started thinking, 'Before we weave, we should have a plan.' So we don't work free-form anymore. Now when we get an order, we make a layout, measure the distance from here to there, and then start weaving. Everyone in our association shares in the overall design of the rug.

"We also wanted to get away from copying the old rugs, with everybody doing the same thing. So now each weaver will do something from her own head. The rugs are black and white in the Beni-Ouarain style, but the motifs in black are all different. Each woman creates her own."

And so the women have moved from traditional "free-form" weaving to a fixed idea of the final article, obeying certain rules about layout and measurement, and at the same time relying on creative inspiration to weave individual designs.

The founder of Anou wants to encourage creativity in Moroccan artisans, a delicate proposition, and one step in doing so has been to provide a training in it for the four artisan leaders. After this training, Kenza designed and produced a very nontraditional rug.

Despite her interest in the new, Kenza is one of the few women

Opposite: A traditional flatweave rug, showing the richness of Middle Atlas weaving.

with insight into the cultural significance of traditional designs. One set of symbols, Kenza says, are the letters of the Berber alphabet, which women "hid" in their weaving, which is where researchers found them. While the alphabet may be very old, the use of it is quite recent in Morocco and not very widespread. The letters are neither Western nor Arabic but look a bit like hieroglyphics. Berber or Amazigh speakers are very proud of them. More generally, Kenza says, "The designs are connected to a woman's life and work. For example, there's one design that represents a horse's bridle. It keeps the horse's mouth closed, it controls. When the design originated, women were dominated. The man was everything. So the design is related to men's control over women at that time.

"The zigzag design we call the 'saw' exists in relation to wood. Like the relationship between saw and wood, we always find the relationship of the man and the woman going along together. Neither could work alone; they help and complete each other." In contrast to the symbolism of control above, here we see interdependence.

"Nature is the source of our colors: the pastel colors of flowers, the green of the grass, and the blue of the sky. The old rugs had orange and blue and purple. We also used mauve, the color we call 'the pigeon's neck.' We didn't often use red, because red is a symbol of blood."

Some designs also come from nature, like the turtle. "Our weaving always has a relationship to nature, to the environment. For the turtle, it's like the woman photographs it in her brain; it's like she copies it.

"As for our religion, the Quran doesn't tell us how to weave, but our work involves certain religious customs. When we wind the warp, the woman has to be ritually clean so that God will help her. The loom is sacred, something we pray over, so it must be kept pure. When we want to anchor the loom we say, 'In God's name, we rely on God.' God's name comes before anything else. The old weaving songs were about God.

"Some women make small prayer rugs. When you pray you should be close to the ground, because we are from the earth and to her we will return. What's essential is that the rug be kept clean because the place where you pray should be clean and pure and good."

Weavers of the Tithrite Association pause while working together on a rug.

For most women, the cultural significance of weaving is far less important than the economic benefits. Kenza joined her first nonprofit development organization when she was attending high school in the larger town of Boulemane. Fortunately, her father did not object to her participation in a mixed group of boys and girls.

"He raised us well, gave us freedom, and taught us to value ourselves. He welcomed my friends, girls and boys, into our home. He knew it's not an association or co-op that will cause bad behavior. Because our father trusted us, I didn't disappoint him. And so I continued my association work."

When the first association began in Ait Hamza in 2001, Kenza became the first woman member; seeing her, others joined. Soon after, she was encouraged to start a local cooperative. Women who had previously suffered exploitation at the hands of an unscrupulous buyer were clamoring for greater independence. Another reason for forming a cooperative: "The women in this area were already accustomed to helping one another weave blankets and rugs for the house. While they worked they talked, made fried bread, applied henna, did a lot of happy things."

Starting a co-op was not easy. First of all, the women decided to move ahead without government support. The trouble was, they didn't know how—a common problem for rural women. "Everyone was saying, 'You need to form one,' but nobody showed us how." Finally a Peace Corps staff member from Rabat told the women how to apply to be a formal co-op. Officials with the Artisan and Cooperative Ministries came to visit them, and in 2003, they founded a co-op called Asma.

Kenza became secretary and then president of Asma, but after four years she left because of health problems. By then she had other ideas about running an organization. "We had to avoid monopolizing things and instead welcome new people to work with us, and we had to bring someone in to check the accounting. I also realized that we couldn't attain our original goals and needed a new direction. In May 2008, we founded an association."

In Morocco, associations differ from co-ops in that associations spend a portion of their time and their income helping the community. The association's first project was sponsoring circumcisions for needy boys. Next they held environmental workshops and helped clean up the village. Because they spent all their funds on the circumcision program, they had no money left for raw materials. Instead, each woman had to bring her own wool. With that wool, the group produced four flatweave rugs, which they showed as samples at local exhibits.

In addition to weaving, the association tried several sidelines. Some women raised goats, but that did not work out. They produced a special couscous, but the grain did not dry during the cold winter months. They learned to make breadbaskets out of recycled plastic and palmetto fibers, but they didn't sell.

Things changed when a local businessman asked them to make fifteen bags with his company logo on them. Money from the sale supplied the association with enough capital to buy wool. After working together on the project and meeting regularly at literacy classes, the group decided to rent a common workspace.

There was still the matter of marketing their rugs. "We'd go to exhibitions and sell nothing at all. Once we went to an exhibition in Marrakesh and sold one pillow. We were put next to the famous Jemaa el Fna Square, and tourists walked right past us. Then shop owners would come and offer us half our asking price. Now we only attend exhibitions when our travel expenses are covered.

"We used to go around to all the weekly markets, but the only

The top row shows the *jrana* (frog) design with a border of *menjel* (scythe) and larger scythe below. The large diamonds are "closed Arab," sometimes also called beads, and the center vertical toothed zigzags are *menshar* (saw).

Left: A neighborhood in Kenza's village of Ait Hamza.
Right: A palmetto grass rug unique to Khemisset, but previously also made in Ait Hamza.

buyers are the middlemen. They'll buy a rug for $16 and sell it for $160 or $315. That happens a lot! The woman receives no profit from her work. Once we sold through a bazaar in Fes, and the owner left us losing money. We barely covered our basic materials. There was nothing for labor or transport. We were just starting out, and didn't understand how things worked.

"At first, we didn't count the yarn or time or anything, and we were eating into our start-up capital. From the association, the women have learned to wait for a decent price. The sale price takes into account the size of the rug, the cost of our materials, and our labor, which amounts to only $2 or $3 a day. We still haven't reached our goal of $5.25 a day [about what a manual laborer earns]. Fortunately, we now have the Anou online site to sell our production, and that's really encouraging us. You don't have to rely on some middleman, and people can learn about our craft and all the stages it goes through."

The way the association handles earnings is different from other groups. When a rug sells, the association gets half and the weaver gets half. The association finances raw materials and travel expenses. Any additional funds support health, education, and environmental activities in the community. Women's earnings range from $37 to $160 a month, but those sales are not constant. After the weavers contribute toward the rent for the workspace ($1.60 a month per person), they spend their income on household expenses, medicine, and schoolbooks. "Children's needs are a priority," Kenza says. "Women spend twice as much on their families as men, who tend to splurge on coffee and cigarettes."

In fact, many women do more than just help out. "There's Itto, whose husband is sick and doesn't work much anymore. She works more than he does and pays all of her son's high school expenses. What does her husband buy? Bread, oil, and sugar. Some women don't have a husband or parents, and they have to support themselves. A woman who supports herself can hold her head high." And several village women do support themselves by weaving.

Itto adds: "We want our weaving to receive the value it deserves. Most people don't appreciate our work. They exploit us. But these rugs are how we live and how we help our children."

Kenza voiced some broader aims. "We hope that our project will grow so that a woman can buy whatever she wants. A woman doesn't only want clothes. She'd like a pretty house finished in glazed ceramic tile. And to have a box where she can keep savings so if she gets sick she can take care of herself. If her husband is standing on the corner waiting to get chosen for a job and works one day but not the next, at least she'd have money for an emergency. These are things we'd like to achieve."

There are now twenty members in the association. The women would like a bigger place to work and not have to pay rent. They'd also like to acquire standard equipment. The looms they brought from home have upright beams made of wood, whereas more professional weavers use metal uprights that offer more consistent tension. The women have squeezed four working looms into their small work area. Aside from needing more space for themselves, expansion would give them a chance to teach more girls and women the craft.

Marketing rugs and earning good money is the key to the future. For Kenza, "the future is this craft. Personally, I hope I can continue my education. To do that, I need money."

She speaks for all the women when she says, "We hope that the Tithrite ["Star"] Association will be a bright star in our village. Being included in this book is an important way for our weaving to find its place and become better known inside and outside of Morocco so that our members, their daughters, and all the women in Ait Hamza will benefit. If a local girl reads about us, then she'll want to produce rugs. She'll say, 'Someday someone will write about me.' The book will give us a history, the beginning of the history of weaving in Ait Hamza. Then we can finally say we've begun to do something. Everyone has some knowledge to share, and it's good if people can benefit from the knowledge of those who went before them.

"Weaving is a symbol of power. Weaving teaches patience. It also gives a woman self-confidence. Even if you make a mistake, you can start again. At first, weaving was just something I liked to do, but it became something that I love. It's like I found out who I really was. I found my true self in weaving."

Kenza's love of weaving is channeled into her village association. While other groups in this book help their members by increasing their income, the Tithrite Association goes further and helps the whole village. Kenza is deeply invested in development, through the efforts of the association and also in her role as an artisan leader in Anou, the innovative online website and national cooperative that allows many Moroccan artisans to sell directly from their smartphones. Her dedication is clear when she voices her ambitions for herself. "I hope to study languages and to do something for my country, so that even if I die, even if I may not marry and have children, people who come after me will say, 'Kenza did this, God's mercy be upon her. She did something for her country.' And I'd also like to help the women whom I work with. We help each other to reach our goals."

Flatweave rug of the Tithrite Association in Ait Hamza.

RURAL FEMINIST AND POLITICIAN

KHEIRA ILAHIANE IS OPENING NEW PATHS for Moroccan women, even though she lives in a traditional rural area. She holds a master's degree and speaks English. Forty-one and single, she is committed to improving socioeconomic conditions for women through community action and to expanding women's roles in politics. She also has a dedication to preserving traditional crafts stemming from her lifelong experience as a weaver. Her eldest sister, Fatima, is a master weaver (page 100), and the contrast in their lives shows the difference a generation can make in the changing culture of Morocco.

After graduating from university in Fes, Kheira returned to her birthplace, Zaouit Amelkis, an oasis village in the Ziz River Valley of southeastern Morocco. There the houses are clustered against dry cliffs, but the land is green, irrigated by the Blue Spring of Meski. Her family raises date palms and also runs a guesthouse. Built of adobe in the traditional southern style, it offers tourists all the modern comforts of home. Kheira lives there with several of her sisters and one nephew. They run the guesthouse and Kheira is the manager.

All of the women in her family weave, and Kheira is no exception. For six years, she wove and sold rugs through a small export company. In a major shift, she began working with two nonprofit organizations: a French-Moroccan association that helped children with disabilities and a group dedicated to women's rights and environmental issues. Loyal to her roots, she went back to weaving, this time working on a project with an inspired mission. The goal was to encourage young women to learn crafts on the verge of disappearing. Older women would get together and teach rug weaving, plaiting palmetto grass to make tradi-

The oasis overlooked and farmed by the village of Zaouit Amelkis.

tional bread containers, and embroidering the black cloaks worn by women in this area. "We were helping each other to preserve our heritage. We didn't want these local traditions to die out. We wanted to revive them, and we hoped the younger generation would work on these products and sell them." Unfortunately, the project lacked sufficient funding to pay its older women as instructors. And the girls said no, they wanted to learn machine embroidery and use knitting machines. "They said, 'We don't want to make rugs or breadbaskets or any of this old stuff. It's just for old ladies.'" This kind of attitude undermined the project, as it has so many similar efforts to protect traditional crafts, and after two years, Kheira gave up.

In 2009, Kheira turned her attention to politics. That year King Mohammed VI established a quota system to increase the number of female representatives in Parliament as well as on the scores of city and village councils. Encouraged by the king's mandate, Kheira stood for election to the village council.

"I had no experience, but I decided to take part in this experiment, whatever happened. If people wanted to laugh, okay; if they wanted to weep, okay; I didn't care. I wanted to represent women. The king gave us the right. 'Let's take it,' I said. 'It's a start.' In a surprising upset, nearly all the villagers voted for me! And the men in the race didn't like it."

But the voters stood by her. They wanted women in government, new people who would work on their behalf. Following the election, two women took seats among the thirteen men on the village council.

Kheira was a member of the minority party, and though council members expected her to oppose programs favoring certain constituents, Kheira wanted what was best for the whole community. "Whether you voted for me or not, I've arrived here and won, so I have to work for everyone, whoever they are." She was especially willing to put aside political differences for programs affecting women.

"When I got on the council, I put up with everything, people fighting with me, people insulting me. They installed streetlights for my neighbors, but not for me. I'm the only one in the dark. They're stuck in being contrary, fighting and suing one another and blocking programs that would help the citizens."

In spite of these conflicts, Kheira ran for the council again in 2015 and won another six-year term. Because of her example, other village women ran for office and won. Now there are four trusted women on the governing body.

In addition to serving on the council, Kheira started working with associations again. She founded a group to encourage environmental tourism, and its male members appointed her as president. Things went well for a year, but then she ran into problems. Some members began rejecting her proposals. Worse, they

made underhanded deals, in the name of the association, that only benefitted themselves. Kheira filed a complaint against them and withdrew as president, although she remains a member of the association.

A similar problem occurred when the male members of an agricultural cooperative invited Kheira to join and serve as their president. At first it seemed like a milestone. But Kheira saw beyond that. "They would just sit there and I'd be working for them. 'Go get this, fix that.' No!" She finally agreed to serve as secretary.

A thoroughly modern woman, Kheira is also dedicated to preserving local craft traditions.

Things went well until the government gave the group a tractor for a project, but the members kept it for their private use. Kheira resigned as secretary and remained the only female member in a group of squabblers.

"I've noticed that the men in associations or co-ops are always fighting among themselves. Who gets between them to solve the problems? Me. If you're in a co-op or association, leave your disputes outside. It's the same problem in the village council. This one fights with that one and they forget to work for the citizens." She's learned that it's easier said than done.

The most traditional group Kheira has worked with is the local tribal council. Village councils, associations, and cooperatives are

The Ilahiane family's inn built against the cliffs outside the oasis.

relatively recent institutions, but up until the 1930s, after which the central government controlled the whole country, the tribal councils were the only bodies that held any real power. Traditional law found in very rural areas still governs their interactions and disputes and in some cases takes priority over national law.

In Kheira's tribe, there are six clans. In 2010, her clan begged her to get involved in tribal matters. Kheira's clan is unique because men and women have equal rights and responsibilities, and women have the right to own land. Recognizing her abilities, her clan chose her to represent them. Kheira became the first woman in Morocco ever to serve on a tribal council.

"In no time, the other clans complained to the local mayor.

'Why did you put a woman on the tribal council?' The mayor explained that my people chose me and that he had no authority over tribal law. But when I met with them over a land problem, one man said, 'We don't want this woman.' The mayor told him, 'It's none of your business to talk about other clans.' But they started in again. They said to me, 'If you stay on the tribal council, we're going to leave this town.' I said, 'Go ahead, leave! Who's making you stay?' We got to the point of insulting each other in public. Finally we found a solution: If there is a problem, the council has to meet in the mayor's office."

Other tribal groups also resented the presence of a woman. When a dispute developed over land boundaries with an adjacent tribe, the authorities called both groups in. Members of her tribe didn't understand the problem, and so Kheira took the floor and announced that it wasn't worth fighting over a few acres. The other tribe turned around and accused her tribe of trying to cheat them. More than that, they questioned her role as tribal spokesperson. "'No, don't talk!' they said. 'Who are you?' I told them I was the same as the others and we each represent 300 or 400 people. I wasn't about to let them destroy my rights."

One of the men who was taunting her didn't even know the borders of his own tribal land. Kheira had done research, talked to elders, and collected information on the land problem. "We don't need to fight," she suggested. "Hire a topographer. He'll tell you by the centimeter." The council finally invited a committee from Rabat to deal with the land issue. A tribal member told Kheira to make lunch for the visitors, which she did, and afterward she told the group, "'Look, I talk on your behalf. I solve the problem. I make you lunch. And you say a woman isn't worth anything!' To this day, they find a woman's involvement hard to bear. Just a few accept us."

However, other tribes have heard about her, and she meets with their representatives to discuss vital local projects such as installing potable water systems. Sometimes they ask her to talk to the mayor or the governor. They've seen what she's done and know it's not just talk. "I came to represent people, in front of God. I have a responsibility, I'm not just playing around."

As the first woman on a tribal council, she was to be televised on International Women's Day, March 8, 2010. Due to technical problems, the program did not air until Women's Day in 2014. After that, many women called or came to visit her. "They'd say, 'God bless you. Now we can speak up. After we saw you, we aren't going backward anymore.'"

During another land dispute, this time in a nearby village, a group of women hired a car and went to see the governor. He met with them, and said, "If women here come to see me with a problem, I have to go and see about it." He went out to the village that very day, and solved the problem immediately. One of the women later came to Kheira's home. "You gave us courage," she said. "That's why we women went to see the governor. We didn't wait for our husbands."

"I said, 'You should just stick to your own nature, and your rights. The king and the law gave them to you. If we wait for men to give us our rights, they won't.' They even tell us that. When I ran in the local elections, they said if it wasn't for the king and the law, we wouldn't let you in."

The woman told Kheira that when she and her neighbors saw Kheira wearing the local black cloak trimmed with colorful embroidery, they started wearing it again. At the same time, they vowed to remove their husbands' turbans, a symbol of manhood. The woman's husband said, "Go ahead, the way is open."

Kheira's high ambitions for women don't always work out. Once she told the members of the village council that if more women were elected, they would have the first all-woman village council in Morocco. "The men said, 'Look lady, enough! Women at home have taken away our façade. Do you want that in the council too? No.'"

But Kheira is generally optimistic about what she can accomplish, and people's reactions encourage her. "I won't forget one old lady who said she'd do whatever she could to help elect me: tell people to vote for me, come with me door to door, on foot and without a penny. When people trust you like that, you're going to work for them. That's enough, that's everything. All the money in the world wouldn't make someone come and thank you like that."

A young woman who received a marriage proposal before she finished high school refused her suitor, saying, "I want to be like Kheira." Kheira was pleased to hear that she is a role model for young women opting for education over early marriage.

Kheira at her sister's loom.

Kheira believes that women have improved their lot, but need more initiatives. "Women should be helped with credit and loans. We can show them ways to earn money instead of relying on handouts or charity. We'll teach them to work and sustain themselves. If you're a woman with a craft, why sit around waiting for the grave? Instead, do something that people will respect you for. It would be like leaving a book for posterity.

"For me, men and women are equal. We both work, we help each other. There's no reason to stay stuck in that old mentality. Thank God that the king gave us our rights. And praise God that we're going to go further."

MOTHER OF THE LOOM

AS FATIMA ILAHIANE TELLS IT, weaving is a metaphor for the sacred and for the circle of women who bind her community together. After years of practice, she gladly passes on the techniques and customs associated with her craft. In fact, her work as a weaver and teacher is an obsession.

Fatima's loyalty to traditional ways stands in sharp contrast to her sister Kheira's fiery activism on behalf of women's rights. Yet in the context of the changing world around them, Fatima's unshakable commitments are just as courageous. When her mother was dying, Fatima promised that she would care for her seven younger siblings. She was married then and had no children, and her husband divorced her when she took on her charges. Since her mother's death she's devoted herself to raising her four brothers and three sisters, including Kheira, the youngest. Everyone in the family calls her Mama.

Mama lives in the village of Zaouit Amelkis, near the thick walls of the fortress-like "adobe condo" that used to protect villagers against violent raiding parties. No one lived in the surrounding oasis, where people grew date palms, olives, wheat, animal fodder, and vegetables. After the marauders were suppressed in the 1930s, villagers began to build individual homes outside the adobe walls. Mama,

Opposite: Fatima Ilahiane working at her loom.
Right: The seating area in the inn near the windows is one for which Mama plans to make a rug.

Kheira, and their sisters now run a comfortable bed-and-breakfast overlooking the fertile oasis. The family's ability to bridge traditional and modern lifestyles is evident in Mama's devotion to time-honored weaving practices and Kheira's work in politics and running a bed-and-breakfast.

"I learned weaving when I was born. When I opened my eyes, I opened them on the loom. From the time I was on my mother's back, I was watching what she did."

As her mother's helper, she had no time for school. Instead, she picked the sticks and thorns out of newly shorn wool and wound warp threads into balls. This was typical for the oldest daughter who became her mother's assistant. Contrast this with Kheira, the youngest girl, who not only went to school locally but went to university and has a master's degree.

Mama knew how to weave before she was married, and she was married before she reached puberty. "I married young, and at first I was scared. I didn't want to part from my siblings or my mother, and I'd keep crying. At least my parents taught me what I needed to know to run a home. I worked with my mother, and we made tents, rope, pillows, belts, blankets, jellabas, and women's capes."

In Mama's tribe, the Ait Atta, a mother has to make two capes for each marriageable daughter in the standard colors of red, white, and black. "There isn't a bride who goes to her new home without something woven."

When making a cape for a little girl, weavers also abide by local custom. "For the first

quarters and plans to weave more rugs plus upholstery and pillow fabric for the public rooms as well.

For her, the work is not a chore. "Weaving gets into your blood and keeps you busy. I'm always working on some design. I have to finish it, to see how it will come out, and then try another one. I don't want to leave it, and the happiness it gives me doesn't leave me either. I get up in the morning and pray, and then I go right to work."

"It's the Internet of the old days," Kheira jokes.

"You don't go out in the sun, you don't go out in the wind. It's not like harvesting olives, gathering fodder for the animals, or milking cows. You're nice and warm inside, you don't have to go out in the cold. If someone invites me to visit, I say, 'No, I'm busy with weaving.' If it's a holiday, people say, 'Don't work, come to our house.' And I say, 'If you want me, come sit beside me at the loom.' Sometimes my kidney stones bother me and I say, 'Ooh ooh ooh,' and the family says, 'Get up from the loom.' But I don't. I lie down next to it and get up and weave when the pain passes."

Mama can't leave the loom empty overnight. If she cuts off one rug, she has to start another or she gets a headache. When the loom is full, she's happy. She'd rather buy wool than meat. "If I eat the meat, it's gone. But a half a kilo of wool makes a pretty rug. Yes, my life is weaving. I really like it a lot. If my health allows it, I will never stop."

Above: Mama with her wedding cape, hung on the wall of their family room. The red is quite faded; it may have been made with dye from madder root.
Right: Mama's daughters: Kheira (center) and her two sisters who run the B & B.

tiny cape, you don't buy wool or use your own supply. You tell people you're making one and say, 'Give me what wool you can,' and each person will give you a little wool. It's so God will make things easy for her. She'll wear it and be protected from rain, she'll wear it while out cutting fodder or taking grass to the sheep. And she'll receive sustenance from God." The same process is followed for a little boy's first jellaba.

Mama only weaves items for her family. "Right now I promised to furnish the house myself, with my labor, my wool, and my loom." She has already completed several rugs for the family

Methods for preparing wool have changed over the last fifty years since Mama started weaving. One process that has largely disappeared is a way of cleaning wool and protecting it from insects. "We'd cook the wool in hot water, which doesn't hurt it. We didn't use soap. In those days, we'd cook it in a pail over a charcoal brazier, and stir it with stick. We'd put it in a cane basket and take it to the river, pull it apart to clean it, and dry it on the sand. Next we'd bring it home and spread it out on the roof to dry. Then we'd clean it by hand again and give it to my mother to card." In some older Moroccan rugs the wool has beautiful sheen, rarely seen in recent rugs. It is probably due to this process, rather than the current trend of just washing the wool using a detergent.

When Mama cards the wool, she separates it into three different grades: the finest wool for the warp, the thicker wool for the weft, and a size in between. All these threads come from one breed of

A line of camels plies the desert near an oasis south of Zaouit Amelkis.

sheep. "You card it to get out the nice warp thread and set it aside. That kind of wool is tough and doesn't break. The warp is everything in weaving." They sometimes add a little goat hair to make it stronger. "When you get it all spun and plied and wound into balls, you grind up a few dates, put them in a pail of water, add the warp balls, and let them soak for a day or two. When you beat the wool as you're weaving, it won't split. It absorbs the water and gets stronger. The wool has to drink.

"Cooking it first protects it. But women don't cook the wool anymore. They take it to the river and wash it with Tide. In the past, if they didn't want to cook it, they used green clay and left it on the wool for two or three days. But with cooking, you don't worry about moths. It's the best thing for wool."

Left Top: The full loom after it has been warped and a rug begun.
Left Center: Heddle threads seen from the back of the loom.
Left Bottom: A finger joint is two centimeters.
Right Top: The border on a bread cloth to protect against the evil eye.
Right Center: Stones used to form a round design on the tie-dyed bread cloth.
Right Bottom: The "puller" used to keep the rug edges straight.

"After the rug is woven, we wash it once a year in the river or the irrigation canal." The canal flows right past the inn, and several women help. They use Tide or shampoo, a brush, and a squeegee to push extra water and dirt out of the rug. Pile rugs are very heavy even when dry and therefore are difficult to handle when wet. The women drape them over a wall and let them drip, then drain them and hang them up.

Mama is the only weaver I've met who has worked with goat hair. When she was small, she, her mother, and her grandmother would visit the nomadic tribes who herded camels, sheep, and goats, and they'd make tents for them of goat hair. It is rarely woven these days because Morocco's nomadic population has dwindled and those who still herd animals in the spring and early summer move to permanent homes in late summer and winter so their children can attend school. "We used goat hair for tents because it's waterproof, for ropes and saddle bags because it's tough. But you can't weave goat hair alone. You have to mix it with sheep's wool using wool combs, and you don't cook goat hair first like you do sheep's wool."

Once the wool is cleaned, combed, and spun, Mama dyes it. She gets red dye from madder root, which grows in the oasis across the road from her house. She says the more you use, the brighter the red. It's sometimes sold in markets as a medicinal tea for treating anemia. She also uses pomegranate rind, walnut bark, and turmeric root, either alone or blended together to produce a variety of colors. "You experiment to see if you get the color you're looking for. And you wash it to see if it runs on your skin or your clothes. It's a lot of work. I learned from my mother, God rest her soul. Of course, there are many colors of sheep's wool too: black, light gray, dark gray, and brown."

Mama is an expert on the traditional way to dress a vertical loom and on the customs associated with the various steps. When she started weaving, looms were built of wood and were planted in the ground to stabilize them. They had to be weighted with stones, and Mama was always standing up and tightening the stabilizing rope. And they were so narrow it was impossible to make a rug wider than 1.5 yards, which explains the usual width of most Middle Atlas flatweaves. The newer metal looms are wider and sturdy enough to allow the weaver to stretch and fold or roll the rug as she works.

When it's time to wind the warp, three women come to help, one at each stake in the ground and a third to pass between them and cross the warp threads on each pass to keep them in order. Mama keeps four stakes permanently in place, two for larger rugs and two for smaller ones. But some weavers pound them into the ground each time they make a rug and take them out when they have finished. The stakes are set two to three feet farther apart than the planned length of the rug, because the rug "eats" some of the warp.

"This year two women came to wind their warp, borrowed our weaving equipment, and then went off to work at home. Loaning the equipment gives you blessings." When friends ask to make their rugs here, Mama always helps. And when she needs support, the women come to her house. It's a fair exchange.

There are special rituals associated with winding the warp. The weavers place a dish or breadbasket beside them, and passersby toss in some salt or a few coins. People also offer a prayer, saying "light and easy" so the work will go well, and the weavers reply, "Protect us from sin." Mama prefers it if people say, instead of giving money, "May God help you."

After winding the warp, the women tie one end with a piece of rope so they won't lose the cross and then take it inside to "sew it to the loom." They replace the rope tie with a bamboo pole that will create the shed, or opening that the weft threads pass through, which Mama calls the soul. Then they use white thread to tie each of the warp ends together and to the boards at the top and bottom of the loom.

"You need three women to 'sew' the loom and three to help you fold or roll it. Three sit on the wooden board, one at each end and one in the center, while three people fold. You have to watch them so one end doesn't roll faster than the other. Sometimes you need to start over."

Top: Madder plant and root freshly picked from the oasis.
Bottom: Detail of a small rug Mama made. The main body of the rug is black and white natural wool; the red color is made from madder root.

"After we attach the warp boards to the loom, two of us tie on the heddles. I use a metal rod behind my loom. When you do that, you are planting the soul in the loom. That gives you the married warp threads, or 'householders,' and the 'bachelors.' That's how we work, and it gives us a rug. If there's not a soul in it, it won't work."

The householders are inside a heddle loop, so they "have a house," and the bachelors are outside the loops. The two alternate. Sometimes you put two warp threads in one "house," but there's one bachelor left over. Or there is an extra warp thread that doesn't fit into the alternating householders and bachelors. "There's always one crazy one on the loom. He doesn't have a house or children. His opinion doesn't have any weight. He's useless. And so we have to get rid of it. Whenever you find one, you have to cut it off." Since cutting an extra warp thread could damage the structure of the rug, you wait until it is well anchored, after a yard or so is woven, and then tie it and cut it off.

"If the women have to go home early and there's no time to tie on the heddles, I sprinkle a little flour along the bottom board and say, 'Please, loom, I haven't left you without any dinner.' And once the warp threads have a soul, we give it supper every night after we finish weaving. We feed it wool, not flour. We insert one thread of weft but don't pound it. That's the dinner for the loom, so spirits won't touch it.

"Also, when you're working and it's time to fold the rug, there can't be any men in the house. We tell them to leave. One of the women who helped fold it has to beat in some wool or just touch the beater before she leaves the house. If you don't do that, you'll work and work on a rug and it will never seem to progress."

Traditionally women measured the length of a rug not in yards or meters but by using their fingers and arms. Today they have combined this with the metric system. Finger joints were used to measure the width of stripes in a cape. Now they say each joint is two centimeters. They also measured with a palm span, as some of the embroiderers do, and say that two palm spans equal a forearm or bone. One forearm equals forty-five or fifty centimeters. The forearm measure is still used in N'kob.

"When we finish a rug, we bring water. Again there should be no trace of a male in the house. Even if there's a small boy who's still nursing, we ask his mother to take him outside. We sprinkle water on the warp board, repeat the first verse of the Quran, and say, 'I gave you water to drink in this world, give me water in the other one when I die.' God knows if it's true.

"Then we sprinkle salt on a mirror and cut the rug off. We use salt so the rug will be 'salty' or lively, and the mirror so it will be pretty. When we cut it off, the soul leaves. From the loom it has died. And the soul of the rug is born into your house. It's like the birth of a lamb. Someone may come by and say, 'Congratulations.'"

Weavers tend to start a new rug when there's to be a celebration, such as a christening or a circumcision or a wedding. They want their homes decorated with beautiful rugs. Some women borrow from others, but Mama thinks it's better to make your own. Women can always count on getting help from other local weavers, with no payment involved.

Hiring a weaver involves certain rules of etiquette. "I don't weave to order, but if I were to weave something for you, I'd ask you for the wool and tell you the price for weaving. You'd ask when I'd start the rug, and I'd say when, and then you'd bring me 'the loom's lunch.' It's like a good deed, and it's not part of the price. You can bring two or three loaves of bread, a little vegetable stew, a little sugar, a little tea. It could be enough for the weaver's whole family or just two, whatever you can afford. As I said, I don't weave for others, but if you asked me to make a rug, it would be like one I'd make for myself, or better. If I couldn't, I wouldn't do it.

"Making a beautiful rug depends on many things. Is the work tight or not? Is it pure wool or not? Will the dye run or not? The rug should also be long enough. You have to measure the area where you want it, but you always need to add a little because it never comes out exact. Something 'eats' it. For example, if I want a four-yard rug, I need to use enough warp for five yards.

"You also need to pay attention to the sides of the rug." Mama and Kheira show me something they call a "puller." "It's how you protect the width of a rug. If you don't keep pulling the edges as you work, it may shrink." In the village of Ben Smim, I saw a metal one, and heard they were getting hard to find. Mama's "puller" was improvised with dowels and knitting needles.

"When you start to work on a rug, glory be to God, he shows you the way. You do a design, then say, 'No, not that one. I'll take it out, I prefer this one.' Even if undoing it is a bother."

Traditional rugs include diamonds and dots of natural dye. Mama also creates "picture" rugs, which are unusual in Morocco. For instance, one might contain images of the world around her: sheep and goats, children on donkeys, and palm trees with golden dates on them.

The women's cape, on the other hand, is changeless. Kheira explains, "This design is customary for our tribe. If you don't do it just right, people will say you missed something. The design is well

Goat hair tent roof panel at the open air market in Khemisset.

known, and you can't add or subtract. If you see ours, you'll know immediately we're members of the Ait Atta tribe. The Ait Hadidou use the same colors, but they vary a little."

One small difference is how the sequins are attached. Mama attaches hers as she weaves while others sew them on after the cape is finished. This would not be noticeable but could affect the structure of the piece, especially for tourists who like to cut off the sequins. They obviously haven't seen them sparkling in lantern light or heard them jingling as a woman walks.

Mama also weaves Middle Atlas pillows with intricate designs. "For those, you have to count, and if you miss one thread, you have to undo it."

She's heard that weavers who work in rug factories use designs drawn on paper, but she's never used a written design. "If you gave me a plan like that, I wouldn't know what to do."

"I do things from nature, things that I see around me, like a sheep or a donkey or a palm tree or a tent." Once she wove a pile rug with their luxurious inn on it, but she sold it, reluctantly, to some neighbors.

Then she showed me a design that has a deeper meaning (see page 104). It resembles chain-stitch embroidery and runs along the edge of a red cloth used to cover bread as it rises. This item (a *mendil*), which is unique to southern Morocco, is usually about two or three feet square and the weave is loose. It is often decorated in a circular tie-dyed design done by tying a string around stones before applying the color. The symbolic pattern frames the bread cloth as well as the borders of some rugs and is believed to protect the owner against the evil eye.

"Working with wool brings blessings! It makes God happy and He thanks you. You don't talk about people or sleep and waste time, and if you weave and earn money, you can support your children with it, and there are blessings in that. I just stay home. If someone comes to see me, I don't say 'Sit down.' I say, 'Come and work to learn. I don't want you to come and just watch me. Learn so you can make your own rug or cape or bedding for your children.' That's what makes me happy.

"Being a good weaver—yes, they sing her praises! Weaving furnishes your house, it clothes you. Isn't that goodness or bounty? What's better, to have a rug you made yourself or to go out and buy it? However nice it may be, it's not like something you made yourself. That's priceless.

"When a girl is going to get married, we bring long sheep hair used to make the warp. It's the quality or the soul of the wool, a symbol of goodness or plenty. At the wedding, we put henna on the bride's hands, and after she's changed and ready, she gets up on a mule to go to her husband's house. Then we wind the long sheep hair on her hands and feet, wrapping each finger and toe. She goes to her husband's house like that. It means she has wool in her hands, she knows or will know how to work wool, and she will have bounty. If a person has wool and a cow, she's well off.

"And so I tell the girls and women to come and I'll teach them to weave, for free. I say, 'I'll come and dress the loom with you in your house. I'll work with you as much as I can.' Some do come. But others don't want to work anymore. They tell me, 'Why should I work on a loom? I'd rather buy a machine-made blanket at the market, that's easier for me.' Very few want to learn. I say, 'Come over', and they say, 'Oh, auntie, that's the work of old ladies.' I remember when my grandmother made a cape for me when I was three years old, and women contributed the wool. It was nice like that. I've taught so many people. And now they say it's the work of old ladies. Only one or two come to my classes."

Kheira continues: "We tried to organize a project to make rugs with local women and sell them abroad, but it didn't last. We tried to set up an association of weavers, but that didn't work out either. But even though the girls who came don't sell their work, they still weave rugs for their homes. That way they pass their time and produce something pretty.

"You see, there are so many pressures working against weaving today. Girls and boys are going to school. The boys don't work in the fields anymore, and the girls don't cut fodder. It's always school, and the portable phone. School has really distanced girls from cooking and housework and crafts like weaving and embroidery. If you look around you'll notice that embroidery is mainly done by girls who dropped out of school. They go home and wait until some bridegroom comes along and asks for them in marriage, and so they embroider a big sheet for their wedding. Others just buy the souk embroidery. Really, you can buy everything. It's not the same as handmade, but people get by with it. They don't value

Perfectly aligned goats for sale in the market.

handwork anymore. They don't want to make rugs. They don't want to stay home. They want to go out and about. Or they sit at home and watch TV. They've even started to buy bread!"

Kheira throws up her hands. "Who knows? Maybe weaving will remain among really dedicated weavers like Mama. Even if you hit her on the head, you'd still find her weaving!"

"It's true," Mama laughs. "People have gotten lazy. Wool gave you a place to live—the tent! Wool provided housing and clothing and furnishings—everything! It was the most important thing in life. It was like food, like wheat. As the proverb says, 'Everything passes away except wheat and wool.'"

SAMIRA BENAYAD

A HEAD FOR FASHION

LONG HOODED ROBES FOR WOMEN may appear limited in style, yet they come in every color of the rainbow and with a lavish array of buttons and rich passementerie. From year to year, the everyday jellaba undergoes subtle changes in fashion. Hems go up and down, waistlines are accentuated or loosened. Fringed trim is in, polyester out, comfort a matter of age or occupation. Depending on taste and trends, the dominant palette shifts, as do the styles and hues of matching or contrasting buttons and embroidered trims. In short, this standard article of clothing that has been around for decades is as steady as the sun and as variable as the desert wind.

The jellaba was originally a liberating garment, freeing women from the yards-long *haik*, basically a long white cloth draped around the body and over the head. The haik was hard to keep on and move in, and so in a bold stroke during the World War II era, women started wearing men's jellabas, which are tailored like a coat and much easier to wear. In the 1960s, they were usually made of *tergal*, a heavy French-made polyester, and came in drab colors like black, brown, navy, and olive green. Times have changed: today's jellabas are slimmer in cut and come in a myriad of machine-made fabrics, colors, and styles, including some that are a foot shorter than the traditional ankle length.

In an age of greater mobility, jellabas are eminently practical garments. They fit most everyone and are loose enough to wear during pregnancy. A woman can toss it on over a plain housedress and go out to visit friends, go shopping, or ride a motorbike and look perfectly proper.

Party dress is a different matter, since it gives every woman a chance to shine even brighter. Qaftans are elaborate long gowns made in luxurious brocade or velvet and embellished with intricate trim down the front and around the neck, sleeves, and side slits. The *teqshita* is two pieces, a qaftan topped with a sheer overlayer, sometimes called a *defina*. The overlayer, made of lace or a subtle print matching one of the colors of the qaftan, also has elaborate trim and sometimes embroidery. The trim is chosen to highlight the fabric and made to order from rayon thread. Women wear these outfits to weddings, circumcisions, naming ceremonies, and other traditional celebrations as well as for special secular events.

Men are mainly stuck with brown or gray jellabas often woven in wool, but they can be attractive if they are made of handspun and woven wool. Sometimes they have stripes in natural colors, and in the Middle Atlas region near Azrou, they are dark brown with a small white overall pattern, reminding one of snowflakes. There are a few articles of more elaborate clothing that were found in remote parts of the country.

Sometimes men wore capes of various kinds: *akhnif* is a man's cape woven to shape, including a curved bottom edge and an attached hood piece. The best-known ones were black with a red "eye" on the back, and other designs woven in. Very few women now know how to weave the curved edge. The ones now produced are made for tourists or collectors. *Aznag* and *aheddoun* are both men's capes woven as rectangles and later cut into a curved shape by a tailor. One woman said the *aheddoun* is made with black and white wool carded together to make gray. Another said they are the same, just with different names, and can be any dark color, though some were brown, made from a dye from a local wood.

Clockwise from top right: Party gowns like those made by Samira. Embroidered slippers for sale in a shop. One of Samira's jellabas with elaborate trim. A two piece party gown with the sheer overlayer embroidered in Fes style by "The Persistent Ones" (page 145). Kebira (page 74) in a jellaba.

SAMIRA BENAYAD LIVES IN TWO WORLDS. An independent, college-educated woman, she found her true calling as a traditional seamstress. Born in a small town, she left her provincial life behind to study economics. After working as an accountant for several years, she fell in love with a pastry chef and is now the mother of a six-year-old daughter and a baby son. In keeping with traditional practice, the four of them live in one room of her husband's parents' house, which happens to be in the bustling tourist mecca of Marrakesh. As the couple and others of their generation see it, living with the family is a convenient way to save money until they can afford a place of their own.

Theirs was not an arranged marriage. Like many other thirty-something women, Samira wanted to choose her mate and marry for love, with the blessings of her family, of course. But how to meet the perfect man in a culture where dating is taboo?

"We met by Internet! That's it. We got to know each other on the telephone. I gave him my number, later he called, and we started to talk, just as friends, nothing else." Their telephone courtship went on for three years. They talked for six months before they ever met. Samira lived in the northern town of Meknes and her husband was in southern Marrakesh, a seven-hour train trip away. He did the proper thing and came to visit her with a group of his friends.

"He wanted to marry from the first. But not me. It's hard to talk about marriage right away with someone you don't know. You need to trust them." After a year, she began thinking about marriage too. "From the first day, he wanted marriage, and he kept insisting until he got what he wanted." When they agreed, they told their families, and his followed the time-honored custom: his mother and sister came to her home with gifts and to formally ask for her hand.

Samira compares the unconventional way she met her husband with the long-established norm: "If I had known somebody without the Internet and he'd come to ask for my hand, 100 percent it wouldn't be like it is with my husband now. For sure it would be worse. Although the way we met was a little strange, not guaranteed, for me it came out better than if it was someone who knew me, like one of our neighbors. I wouldn't find anyone better than

him." She used to wonder what he was like when he wasn't on the phone, when he always sounded happy. "But that was him—he never gets angry. Lots of people have run into problems with meeting on the Internet. But thank God, I was safe. It turned out well. It is hard to find someone."

After the birth of their daughter, she stayed home. One day, her mother-in-law suggested that she help her sister-in-law, who ran a successful sewing business in the family house. The sister-in-law offered to teach her to sew, and Samira decided to try it.

"At first it seemed strange to me. I had never sewed, and it was hard to learn. And, you see, I was educated, had studied, had finished my B.A., and then had a job. To end up sewing seemed like a comedown. But when I sat down at the machine, I liked it. Now I feel content at the machine. I like to sew. When my mother was young, she used to sew on the machine and I used to sit next to her. I liked that skill, that craft of sewing; I liked it in my mother."

Samira was already twenty-seven years old when she became a traditional seamstress. This means she makes traditional clothing like jellabas as well as elaborate qaftans and tqashet. She also produces modern, less formal clothes, such as housedresses and women's sports outfits.

Like most skilled seamstresses, Samira sews for individual clients rather than for shops. Fortunately, she doesn't have to search for customers because her sister-in-law has built up an extensive clientele in the neighborhood. Even though the sister-in-law recently moved to a new home, she still runs the business in the old family house. She rides her motorbike through the narrow streets—one of thousands of "Kesh Angels"—and whenever her bike is parked outside the house, her clients come flocking.

The women are eager to have new custom-made outfits for spring and major holidays, and that's when business is humming. Off-the-rack jellabas are shoddy, and if women can afford a tailor-made garment, they are quick to order it and then pass on the old one to a sister who lives in another town. The endless desire for nice new jellabas creates a good steady business for traditional seamstresses.

Samira makes jellabas for female clientele, who choose the style,

Samira models one of her intricate two-piece gowns. It still fit, though she was expecting her son in a month.

Wool from sheep like these grazing in northern Morocco will be used for wool jellabas.

fabric, and trim. Male tailors make men's jellabas, which come in more subdued colors and fabrics, including wool. (Women used to weave the wool fabric for their husbands' and sons' jellabas, but today the fabric is either handwoven by male weavers or is machine made.) Samira also makes formal qaftans and tqashet. Naturally, these complicated garments are more expensive than jellabas, and

their creation involves several artisans.

The first step is to cut out the garment. Samira's sister-in-law, who has a two-year degree in tailoring, does the cutting. Then Samira sews the garment on her machine. To cover the seams, she uses *kabel,* a thin rayon handmade band that is also part of the trim. On traditional men's jellabas, the pieces of fabric are joined with kabel by hand.

After the garment is stitched, Samira applies the various trims.

A complex design on the front and sleeves is made with a special sewing machine. (In the past, men did the trim by hand.) Then another sister-in-law sews on the buttons, and Samira puts kabel and the ornate trim around them. Another sister-in-law does the final finishing, hemming the robe by hand.

In addition to these four artisans, two others are involved in making this garment: a woman who makes the buttons for the front of the garment (you will meet three of these specialists later in this book), and a man who makes the *sfifa* and kabel trims in the same color but with different designs. If there is to be embroidery, a seventh woman is involved. Samira always works with the same team.

Despite the amount of labor, a jellaba costs about $50, including the fabric. Samira makes $2 to $3 for sewing the garment, $6 for applying the intricate trim, and $2.50 for the finishing. Her sister-in-law calculates the amount each of the artisans will charge, depending on the complexity of the work, and sets the final sale price.

Samira and her sister-in-law follow the latest styles. "Every year, certain colors and models are in fashion. Green, which is always good for parties, was a big deal a while ago. But if I want something now, I'd choose another color. Last year, everyone was wearing yellow and red jellabas. A few years ago, the trim was done in two or three or more colors. But last year, they started using the same color as the jellaba. The whole garment is just one color."

In spite of changing fashion trends, Samira doesn't always follow ever-shifting tastes. However, her current favorite, a gold jellaba, is trimmed in the same color. She likes it because it is light, and the trim is pretty and "simple." In fact, the trim is applied in elaborate curlicues but appears simple because it is the same color as the garment.

Samira likes all her pieces, even those that are less classically elegant. Well, she wasn't entirely pleased with the loose house-dress (*pyjama*) she was wearing, mainly because it was store-bought and not well made. It is this distinction that leads women to buy tailored clothing, especially to wear in public.

Samira appreciates many aspects of her work. "What's nice about it is that I can stay home, wake up in the morning, do my housework, cook the food, and my daughter plays next to me while I sew on the machine."

But as time went by, she began to worry about her income. It was enough to go to the public bath or to buy a jellaba, but not sufficient to help pay the mortgage on their new house.

When they needed more money, Samira decided to go back to her old career as an accountant, and although it didn't exactly fit her education, she accepted a position with a notary handling land

Samira's daughter, Aya, happy at home.

titles. She lasted four months. "There's a boss, and he requires you to do extra, like stay late, to satisfy him. And he delays payment, five or ten days, and you may want to travel or buy something you need."

While working at that office, she heard about a competitive exam for teaching jobs. Morocco has made great efforts to staff rural schools by training university grads as teachers. Samira decided to test her limits, and she succeeded. But before the one-year training began, she grew ambivalent. She spent a long time weighing the pros and cons between sewing and teaching.

In the end, Samira chose the teaching for job security. Teaching offers a guaranteed, lifelong income. However, it means that she has to leave her family for weeks at a time. New teachers are given the least desirable jobs, which are far from the city. Even with seniority, a city posting is rare. Her job is fifty miles from Marrakesh, and the last twelve miles are on a perilous dirt road. It takes more than three hours to drive there, and in bad weather, she has to ride the ruts on a mule. Last year, she came home every two weeks and sometimes took her five-year-old daughter back with her. This year, she comes home every week and doesn't take her daughter, because she's now in school, but she has to take her baby son.

Fortunately, her mother-in-law takes care of her daughter during the day and her husband watches her at night.

The village where Samira teaches is tiny and isolated, with a population of about 200 people. The government provides her housing, and during the week, Samira lives in a one-room house with a kitchen and a toilet. All three teachers live together in that house, because the women are afraid to be alone in such an isolated setting (even though they know there is no real danger). Although the conditions are difficult, Samira enjoys the thirty-six students enrolled in the school, grades one through six.

Samira continues sewing for her sister-in-law during school vacations. And in her spare time, she sews clothes for herself. She's just bought material to make a qaftan and a new jellaba to wear after her son is born, one for the naming ceremony, the other for everyday use. Samira enjoys the part-time seamstress work, but she is willing to take on the difficult aspects of teaching, including the commute, to have a home and a good future for her family.

Samira and her husband pool their earnings and spend most of them on school tuition for their little girl, who attends a progressive French language school. Tuition is high, but Samira and her husband want the best for her. The rest of their income goes toward household expenses. The couple used to keep their money in a closet and take out what they needed. Because Samira didn't limit herself to what she earned, her husband would give her his pay and tell her to use it as she wished. They spent for the house, and Samira planned to spend her own money to go out with friends or to buy a new jellaba.

When Samira was sewing full-time, she earned up to $180 a month. Her sister-in-law, she guessed, earned anywhere between $120 and $360 a month, depending on the season. In comparison, Samira's entry-level teacher's salary is about $600. While her income is much higher than her sister-in-law's, she spent four years getting her university degree and an additional year in teacher training.

Samira views her own worth in a positive light. "If I make my own clothes—how can I say it?—it's good, not like a woman who learned nothing, a woman who just stays at home, cooking, feeding the kids, doing housework. A woman should study, go out, be a little open-minded. Even if I were not educated, rather than just sitting at home, I'd look for a craft to learn and earn a little money. I wouldn't be always saying to my husband 'Give me, give me, give me.' If a woman is financially independent, her opinion has weight; she'll be treated like she has value.

"But," Samira adds, "there are women who have the opposite opinion. They say no, the husband provides things and the woman should be pampered. I am not saying she should go out and clean houses, though that's work too. She could learn some handwork, like my sister Fatima (page 134). She does handwork, so she doesn't need to wait for someone to give her money. If you get stuck, you can work and earn money, not wait for your brother or your husband to give it to you. I prefer to have my own money."

Samira is pleased that she and her husband share their incomes. "My money is his; what he has, he provides—no problem. You have to help your husband. We got married, we want to have our own home, buy furniture. If I just sat around doing nothing, how would that help him? Should I just cook and eat? It's necessary that I help him so we can achieve what we want."

Samira respects women with skills like hers, although she says that some people are jealous of a skilled woman who earns an income. She says only people in her family know she sews, and some of them are envious.

Samira is confident about the future of her craft. She advises any woman who's not educated, who doesn't know what to do, to buy a machine and learn to sew. She feels it's the best craft for a woman who doesn't have a job, because she can help support herself while staying at home. "Some men don't want their wives to go out at all, but the wives could work at home and women clients will come to them. She can do her housework, be with her children, and still make money. A woman won't have to sit

Daily life in the streets next to Samira's home.

around saying, 'I don't have this, I don't have that.' She needs to get moving and do something!" There's plenty of work, she says, especially with traditional clothing. After she learned to sew, at least two young women from closely related families saw that she was making money and they went out and learned too.

As a young, educated artisan, Samira has more options than many women. Although the lower pay is discouraging, she considers sewing an excellent way for less educated women to earn an income. But the money isn't everything. Samira enjoys her craft, the technical challenges as well as the pleasures of creating beautiful items. The field offers another intangible benefit: once a woman contributes to the family economically she will achieve a stronger voice in family decisions.

Samira's independent streak is reflected in many aspects of her life. The unconventional way that she and her husband met, the fact that they share their incomes yet still live in the same home with his parents, and the fact that she maintains two careers, teaching and traditional sewing, along with motherhood and housekeeping, illustrate the changing lifestyles in Moroccan society today.

A GRASSROOTS FEMINIST BUTTON MAKER

THEY RUN DOWN THE FRONT of women's and men's traditional clothing and sometimes surround the sleeves, hundreds of them bubbling from head to toe; it's hard to imagine fastening and unfastening them all. But that's just it; they're meant to adorn as well as serve. They come in a multitude of colors and shapes, and the women who make them have given them names: jacquard, jasmine, chain, watermelon, turbans, noodles, and more.

Like the designs in rugs, buttons are named after objects they are thought to resemble. *Bstilla* refers to a sweet and savory dish made with chicken, ground almonds, saffron, and phyllo pastry garnished with cinnamon and sugar and served at weddings. The resemblance between the button and the pastry is rather obscure, although both are round and flat and the elaborate stitching on the button looks vaguely like pastry crust.

The derivation of the traditional *semma* style is uncertain, but Aziza Bourouaha reasoned it out. "*Semm* is the name of women's slippers embroidered with gold thread. Some buttons are worked in metallic thread. The name probably comes from that."

The buttons are small and difficult to make. The technique, called needle weaving, uses simple tools to produce complex results. Women begin by twisting strands of rayon thread together and then steaming the twisted threads over hot water so that they will not unravel when they are cut. Next, they prepare a core for the button. The core was once made from a tiny scrap of rolled newspaper, but today, most women use a piece of plastic tubing. They place the core on a drill bit, thread a dull needle with the plied rayon, and begin stitching the complex pattern. The first stitches set the "path" for the rest of the weaving.

The basic material is rayon thread. Rachida Ousbigh, whom we will visit later, says, "Some call it silk (*hrir*), some call it *sabra* (Arabic for aloe), but it's the same thing—though it's not real silk. While hrir literally means silk, and although the thread shines like silk, Amina Yabis says real silk was never used for making buttons, not even for the king's family. That was true during her lifetime, but in fact Morocco did its own silk rearing in the nineteenth century, and qaftans before the 1940s had silk buttons. After that, it was replaced by rayon, which took the place, and the name, of silk. Of the different qualities of rayon thread, the best is imported from China. In fact, women don't choose the thread at all. Since buttons are made to order to match certain fabrics, the tailor gives them the thread in the right colors and tells them the style he wants. The rayon is either dyed in Casablanca or comes from China via Casablanca.

Most button makers do this tedious work day after day, because no robe would be complete without many buttons. In the last few years, a few enterprising women have formed cooperatives and gone on to turn these tiny threaded jewels into earrings, bracelets, and necklaces, which means they have to string hundreds of buttons into thick baubles that will grace a woman's wrist or neckline. More buttons, more colors, more work, more coins.

AMINA YABIS IS A LIVELY WOMAN in her early fifties, with sparkling eyes and boundless energy. If you met her on the street in Sefrou, you might assume she was an ordinary housewife, but Amina is far from ordinary. Like many Sefrou women, she makes the buttons that are sewn on qaftans and jellabas. In one of her creative flashes, she transformed those intricate handmade buttons into necklaces, bracelets, and earrings, which she markets in Morocco, Europe, and the United States.

An array of intricately knotted buttons transforms into a colorful necklace.

Amina does so much more! She has organized local button makers into a thriving cooperative that guarantees the women, rather than middlemen, the major profits on sales. She is also the treasurer of a new job-training center for women. Working with Peace Corps volunteers, she has traveled throughout Morocco helping women to set up cooperatives and to learn the use of natural dyes. In these and many other activities, she has gone beyond her own interests to improve the lives of village women. Amina is a grassroots feminist.

Amina was born and raised in an old working-class neighborhood of Fes. Her family was poor, and she had to sacrifice her education to help support her brothers and sisters while they attended school. She worked as an embroiderer, sewing glistening gold patterns on women's slippers and horse saddles. The experience served her well. After she married, she moved to Sefrou and took up button making as a means of helping support her growing family. Amina's husband is a teacher at a rural primary school nestled among groves of olive trees. The couple has four sons, three of whom are married with children of their own. The youngest, who is studying at the university, still lives at home.

Sefrou is known for its olive oil and its buttons. Originally the city's large Jewish population dominated the button trade, supplying tailors in Fes until the 1960s, when they were encouraged to emigrate to Israel. Moroccan author Leila Abouzeid is from Sefrou and learned to make buttons as a child in the 1950s. Her father insisted she and her sister go to school, so her mother enrolled them. In her memoir, *Return to Childhood: The Memoir of a Modern Moroccan Woman*, she writes, " . . . Presumably she was not convinced this was the right path for us to follow, because she took us to learn caftan button-making as well. The making of caftan buttons was a craft of Sefrou women, Muslim as well as Jewish, who were said to be particularly skilled at it."

Before the mass exodus, Jewish women passed on their skills to their Muslim neighbors, and Amina learned button making from them. In nearby Fes, young men acquire training by apprenticing themselves to master artisans who are accredited members of one of the ancient craft guilds. But such a formal system doesn't exist for women. Amina had to find teachers on her own. "I'd see women sitting on their doorsteps, working buttons, so I said, 'Teach

me,' and I learned. At first I just sat next to different women and helped them. I didn't earn any money. After a year, I became good enough to work and to get paid."

Like most women in Sefrou, Amina works on buttons every day, after her housework is done. She needs strong afternoon light, especially for black buttons, because the work is hard on the eyes. There's more work, and better pay, during the summer months when people hold weddings and other celebrations and are anxious to have elegant new garments adorned with beautiful handmade buttons.

"The buttons I like most are the semma buttons, the old ones

Amina gathers wildflowers with children at the school where her husband teaches. She will use the flowers for dyeing fabric.

that the Jews taught us. They're the genuine article. They worked like a button and could last up to fifty or sixty years, even with paper centers and being washed many times. This used to be the only style, but now girls don't learn it because it's difficult. Only the older women make them. That's good for us, because today it's all about old styles. Lots of people come from Rabat and Fes to order them, and even from the king's palace to order them. The royal family's qaftans and tqashet have these buttons."

Amina doesn't care for the new styles, particularly the jacquards,

Children from the rural school where Amina's husband teaches.

which have only been around for five or six years, and wear out rapidly. "They're a fad," she says. "They appear and disappear quickly."

Buttons are sold in bunches of forty. Depending on the height of the buyer, four or more bunches may be needed to run down the front of a jellaba. In the early 1990s, a bunch sold for twenty-five cents. Usually a woman could make one bunch a day, but if she had help, she could produce four bunches a day. In other words, a woman working full tilt could earn as much as a dollar a day.

The tailor supplied the raw material and set the price. His pay-ment was based on the quality of the work and the final sale price of the garment. If a customer was going to pay $50 for a jellaba, the tailor would ask for good-quality buttons and pay the artisan accordingly. If the client chose a $10, ready-made jellaba, the tailor would say, "Just do them any old way," and wouldn't pay much.

Once Amina understood the pricing better, she changed the system, for herself and for many other women. "I went out and saw how much the men paid and how much they profited from women's labor. I told the women, 'You women, the men profit a lot from you, you need to find a way out of that.' And that's the reason why I formed a co-op."

But forming a cooperative wasn't easy. "At first, only single or widowed women participated. Married women didn't join because their husbands wouldn't let them. The husbands said, 'No, don't go, that Amina just lies, she wants to profit herself, she's not a good woman.' But when the men saw me in Sefrou—yes, they watched me, and they knew I went right to work and didn't do anything bad—they finally started to trust me and to send their wives." The co-op was the first in town and began in 2000. There are now about twenty co-ops in Sefrou.

Amina discovered that tailors doubled the price when they sold the buttons. Through the co-op, the women started earning that profit. Soon the women and the tailors were competing for the buttons to sell.

The co-op women were paying five cents more for a bunch of forty, and soon the men raised the price. This went on, in five-cent increments, until it became a real price war. The co-op women decided to buy from women in more rural areas. The trouble was that the men owned their own cars and the women had to pay for taxis. They would rent a big taxi and take materials out on a Monday and

Left: Semma buttons.
Right: Jacquard buttons.

pick up the finished buttons the following week.

The solution came when the husbands told their wives to work with the co-op women, not the tailors. When male buyers used to visit the house, the husbands would go outside and deal with them. But co-op members can enter the house, have tea, and talk. The button makers earn more and enjoy having visitors.

There are now forty-two women in the Cherry Buttons Cooperative, twenty-two in Sefrou and twenty in outlying villages. Now rural women come into Sefrou once a week to pick up and deliver orders. Instead of going out to the countryside, Amina and her coworkers travel to Casablanca and Fes to buy materials and solicit orders. The orders are large; the co-op recently netted over $1000 profit from one commission alone.

Morocco is full of so-called co-ops. But Amina runs a *real* co-op. All members of her co-op, and also nonmembers who help fill their orders, are paid the same amount for the buttons they make, which is now thirty or forty cents for a bunch of forty in the winter, and fifty or sixty cents in the summer. The more the women work, the more they earn. Beyond their button income, the actual members, including those who work as middlewomen, share in the year-end profits. An accountant with the Ministry of Handicrafts helps keep track of sales and profits and calculates each woman's share. Last year, the profits ranged from $200 to $400 per person. Amina received $400, mainly for the time she spent traveling and getting orders.

Buttons named *boushniqa* after the dried flower of Queen Anne's Lace they resemble.

"The women use their income in different ways. Some of them make buttons just to fill their spare hours. They already have money, and with their extra earnings, they travel or buy a new dress. Other women have to work because they need to eat."

Amina falls somewhere in between. "When I came to Sefrou and had small children, my husband accumulated a lot of debts and I needed to help him out. So I learned to make buttons. Every day I got up at 5:00 in the morning, made bread and cooked the meals by 8:00 a.m., and worked on buttons until 5:00 or 6:00 p.m. I did it to educate my sons. My boys had to go to school and play sports so they wouldn't end up in the street and start smoking." She used to pay for her sons' public bath fees, sports fees, and haircuts, because their father couldn't afford it. She also treated them to new clothes for holidays. "I worked hard to make my children happy."

Amina says she brings in about 25 percent of the family's income. But knowing how to make buttons doesn't necessarily earn a woman much respect. "When you ask a woman about her craft, she'll say, 'I just make buttons,' like it's something that has no value. But if a girl or woman is really good at it, that's different. We'll all be sitting around and we say, 'That girl is hadga, she makes buttons really well. If she married into your family, she'd really help her husband.'

"But we have a problem now because girls don't want to learn to make buttons anymore. City girls would rather work outside the home where they have a chance to meet boys. Fortunately, button making won't die out because rural girls and women still make them. It's the only kind of work they have."

Amina's achievements go well beyond her skills at practicing and promoting her craft. Forming a cooperative was the first step in her career as a grassroots feminist activist. Since there is no word for "feminism" or "feminist" in Moroccan Arabic, Amina talks instead about women's rights. How did a woman who grew up in a traditional family with a limited education and limited options become so committed to women's rights?

It was her husband, Si Mohammed, who opened the doors. When they married, he was a member of a Moroccan human rights organization. "He told me, 'We work on women's rights, we defend women's rights, but not one woman comes to our meetings. The men just talk about women's rights—and leave their wives at home. The wife needs to be there too.' Well, from time to time I used to go with him to that association, and if there was some training course, I'd go. I started to learn a little. I was listening and watching."

Amina was a quick learner. The first thing she did was to run for city council in 1994. "I was the first woman to stand for election in Sefrou. I didn't do that to win and get a job. No, I did it to show that a woman has the right to run in elections. She, too, can defend people's rights, and she, too, has the right to stand for election, not just vote." Although she didn't win, many women voted for her.

Amina's experience with the co-op taught her that it offered more than better earnings. "The woman who used to stay home and spend all day in the kitchen, then work on buttons until she went blind, began to go out and see the world. Two of us went to France. Another time, we went to Spain. Those women never imagined they'd go abroad!" Amina has attended the International

Examples of the round design called *shems* which means sun.

Folk Art Market in Santa Fe, New Mexico, where the button jewelry made by her cooperative reaped huge sales. While traveling, she emails and Skypes with family members and keeps up her Facebook page, posting family photos and pictures of herself at international exhibitions.

Her work with the co-op has won wide recognition. Amina was nominated for a Khamisa Award as an outstanding businesswoman in 2006. She was also chosen for a museum exhibit in Santa Fe as one of ten women worldwide whose co-op has greatly helped women.

Although most of Amina's work focuses on economic benefits for women, she sees other needs to be met. "There are still women who aren't able to demand their rights. A woman who needs papers from the administration will say, 'Come with me, Amina. You talk and you raise your voice. When they see you, they will give the paper to us. When they see you, they hurry up.'

"Another woman wanted me to go to the governor's office and ask for a scholarship for her daughter. I told her, 'It's one of your rights! You can go and talk about your daughter, and your daughter, who is in the university, can talk too.' The woman said, 'We can't do that, we're afraid.' Well, the next day I went to the governor to speak for them."

Amina's greatest pleasure is when she sees women learning and going on to help others. "Whatever I learn I teach to other women so they can use it to make a living. That's my work. I give my time and knowledge, and, praise God, later I hear that what I did succeeded. 'Oh, they started a cooperative, they're selling, they went to an exhibition.' This year two cooperatives traveled to the International Folk Art Market in Santa Fe. They learned a lot, and now, God bless them, they are teaching others. That's the kind of thing that makes me happy.

"You know, I've always liked all kinds of handwork. When I was a girl I learned gold thread embroidery. Learning to use thread and a needle changed my life. I didn't go very far in school, because my family was needy and poor. But my craft gave me many things. It helped me with my mother when she got sick. It helped me with my sons. It changed my future and my children's. I never imagined that I could put my son through university, and now he has a master's degree and works for the national phosphate company. Yes, a needle and thread changed my life. That's why I tell women, 'Any kind of work that you do, value and respect it, and it will give back to you.'"

AZIZA BOUROUAHA

A WIDOW'S STORY

WHAT DO YOU DO if you're a traditional Moroccan woman of fifty with no education and your husband dies, leaving you with a young girl to raise alone? Some women move back home with their families. **Aziza Bourouaha** chose another way.

When Aziza was eight years old, her family moved from the small village of Tahar Souk in the Rif Mountains to Sefrou so that her older brother could get a good education. Aziza stayed home and helped her mother; she never went to school or even to a women's craft center. "My parents were strict and wouldn't let me out of the house," she says. Eventually she grew up and married. Her hus-

band worked in a restaurant, but after suffering from diabetes for many years, he died, leaving Aziza with no income and no skills of her own. Her older daughter used to crochet fancy trims, but after having children, she turned to button making as a way of earning some money. Aziza's younger daughter learned to make buttons when she was twelve and still helps make buttons when she isn't studying. Aziza was a late bloomer. At age thirty-five, she learned to make buttons from a neighbor and began to sell them. Now she is always working. "If I don't make buttons, I don't have anything to live on. There's no man to put food on the table."

Aziza has never had to produce the styles and colors dictated by tailors. "I sold my own buttons. I traveled with lots of buttons in lots of colors. I used to sell them in Rabat and Khenifra, in Casa and Meknes, in Tangier, Tetouan, and Oujda. But after a while, I stopped traveling. I got worn out.

"A little later, the idea of the co-op came to us. Amina Yabis and I lived in the same street, and one day we ran into a guy who was on the city council. He said, 'You should start a co-op.' He gave us the idea.

"We asked him, 'How do we make this co-op?' He said, 'Go to the Artisan Ministry, to their local representative, and he'll show you how.' So Amina and I went to his office and said we wanted to start a co-op. He told us you do this, you do that, bring this, do that. He asked if we knew about buttons, and I said yes, I made them. He asked if we traveled and sold them, and I said yes, I go to lots of places. He said, 'Good, you have experience, so now create a co-op.' There was an American woman here then, a Peace Corps volunteer, and she, bless her, helped us out. The local representa-

A collection of Aziza's buttons representing hours of work and also her livelihood.

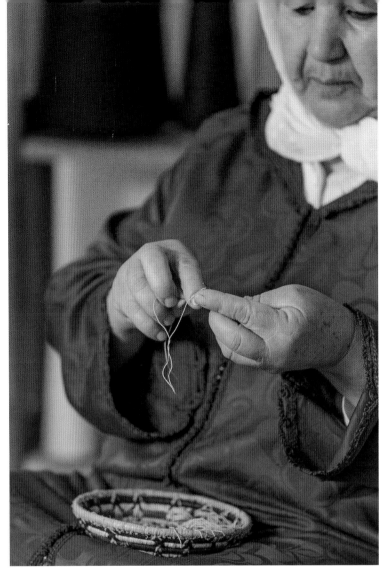

Aziza's daughter Fatima Zahra (left) and Aziza (right) making buttons in their home.

tive helped us too, God bless him. He showed us what to do.

"So we gathered some women together. We guaranteed ourselves and we collected a little money. That American woman, God bless her, gave us some money, too, and stood by us. So we all chipped in and God helped us succeed. I stopped working on my own and I joined the co-op." That was around 1996.

With the initial funds, the co-op members went to Fes and bought rayon thread, which they stored in a government-sponsored craft center in Sefrou. Then they traveled to the surrounding villages and handed out materials to rural women. About three hundred women sell buttons to the co-op but are not among the forty-two members.

"When I joined the co-op, I started sharing with the others.

There was a big difference. Before, I used to get all the profit. Afterward, I'd work and it would go to the co-op. The co-op would do the accounting and each would get her share. We had good benefits. We all worked and helped each other out."

Now she and Amina travel together and sell to merchants, especially in the busy summer season. The women don't ask a price; the merchant tells them what he'll pay. If the women don't like the price, they go to another shop. "Of course, the co-op has competitors who try to undersell us. But the shop owner really knows quality. For good buttons, he gives a good price.

"With my co-op earnings, I buy my daughter's clothes and pay her monthly school fees. I pay water, I pay the electric bill, I buy food. If I had to pay rent, we wouldn't be able to eat." She has even bought braces for her daughter's teeth.

When she started out, in 1986, Aziza made one or two styles of

Perfectly shaped buttons line the sleeves and front of a woman's jellaba.

buttons, which she sold in bunches of forty for fifty cents. Somehow she managed, because "in those days life was cheap."

But then the market started to move. "A lot of new styles came out, and prices for our work went up. Handicrafts came back to life. People put buttons on jellabas and qaftans, lots of buttons, all the way down the front and on the sleeves, and on men's jacket and pant outfits too. So buttons became a good business and were given some importance. There are about fifty or sixty styles now, and the work is really expensive."

Aziza produces a wide variety of buttons out of shimmering, colorfast rayon thread. Like her friend Amina Yabis, she prefers the semma style, mainly because it is traditional and in great demand. Amina turns up her nose at the jacquard button. "It's cheap. There isn't a profit in them, and they've fallen out of fashion." She and Amina use the jacquard buttons for necklaces.

Aziza can make eighty fancy buttons a day and earn $1.50 for a bunch of forty, three times as much as she made in the past. That means she earns $3 a day, which brings in $90 a month. She also earns for her work traveling and selling as a middlewoman, but then she isn't making buttons. Although the income seems low, Aziza is satisfied with the earnings from her craft. And times have improved.

"All the crafts—sewing, embroidery, and button making—are valued," Aziza says. "It doesn't matter if a woman is really good at it. The fact that she is working and earning is the important thing.

"Traditional crafts are good for everyone. If a woman doesn't have a husband, she can work for herself. Poor people can help themselves, they can help their parents. And this craft, button making, will never end. There are handicraft institutes for learning it, and they'll never close. Even if people wear modern styles to work, we don't wear modern clothes to parties. For christenings, weddings, and engagements, we have to wear traditional clothing."

Aziza is a hard-working woman who has stitched together a career with a positive and secure economic future. These little buttons allowed her to raise a daughter on her own, and send her to the university. She may attribute her success to the power of traditional ways, but sees no other relation between her craft and her religion. "Buttons are a craft, and our religion—we need to follow it. Beliefs are one thing," she says, "buttons are another."

WOMEN'S CRAFTS OF KHENIFRA

EVERYONE IN MOROCCO NEEDS BUTTONS, but the women who make them often do better by creating new items, forming an association, and selling their original products themselves. Rachida Ousbigh is one of those women. We first met in the summer of 2014 at the International Folk Art Market in Santa Fe, New Mexico, where she was selling the button-bead jewelry made by her association, Women's Crafts of Khenifra, of which she was the treasurer. As I translated for her during various training workshops, I was struck by this self-assured young woman's love for her craft and the articulate way she spoke about the trials and triumphs of her artisan organization.

A year later, I was driving through fields of spring wildflowers toward her town of Khenifra, in the western foothills of the Middle Atlas Mountains. Khenifra is a medium-sized rural town of about 100,000, with an economy based on herding sheep and raising wheat and barley. Many women weave, and there is a rug market on Fridays and Saturdays.

A single woman of twenty-eight, Rachida lives in her family home. As we sat in the parlor, talking, we were joined by **Fatima Nouaman,** her good friend and the secretary of the association, who added her own bright notes to the conversation. Fatima is also twenty-eight and finished high school. She would have liked to go to university, but there was none in town, so she did not continue. Her education is useful to the association: she keeps track of orders and correspondence on the Internet, and she has a basic command of English.

Rachida has been making buttons for the past twelve years, starting at age sixteen when her aunt taught her the craft. Three

years, later she dropped out of high school and began making buttons full-time for a local tailor. Her life might have followed the norm had not a series of Peace Corps volunteers come along and introduced the idea of stringing buttons into fashion jewelry. They organized and trained a group of women, taught them the basics of running a business, and helped them find markets. After ten years, the women were on their own—and doing very well. Today Rachida's association designs and makes necklaces, earrings, and

Bracelets formed with a variety of button styles.

Rachida Ousbigh with Fatima Nouaman.

bracelets in a variety of styles and colors for clients all over the world. The craftsmanship is superb and the jewelry particularly appealing to Westerners.

Producing hundreds of buttons for each necklace requires constant work. Every day, Rachida picks up her threads and needles, turns on the TV, and stitches away. "Actually I just listen to the TV," she says. "I have my head bent down over a button unless there's a 'good' scene. Then I take a quick peek and get right back to work."

She's especially in a rush when she needs to fill wholesale orders for the summer holidays.

"Really, once you know how to make the jacquard button, the other kinds are easy. You can learn fast and you just need to decorate them. There are lots of styles: jacquard, *bildi* ("country style," or "traditional"), *alkhossa* ("fountain"), *lfrayza* ("strawberry"), *lhakaka* ("scrubber"), and more.

"Every year a new style appears. Then time passes and people go back to the older ones. Right now some new styles are coming out that have never been seen before. Of those new styles, the one that I like a lot is the "acorn" *(beloTa)*. It's hard to make because there are three kinds of designs in it, starting with the basic jacquard. And it has to have two colors so the designs will show up well. I like this style because it holds up over time.

Fatima adds, "These buttons are the traditional beauty of Morocco. People used to use them on men's and women's jellabas, and they keep developing this Moroccan beauty."

Rachida elaborates, "A well-made button should have no ends of the thread showing; they should all be worked in. If a woman's work is loose, if the threads get away from her, if you see the tubing through holes in the thread, it's a defect. If her work is bad, tailors won't buy from her."

Rachida often sees these flaws in the traditional bildi style, which is one of the reasons she dislikes them. "The thread isn't tightly plied, the design isn't great, and it's harder to make than the acorn style even though it has just one design, one color, and is relatively plain. The acorn has two colors and looks pretty. Of course, everyone has her own taste."

Taste varies from place to place. Amina Yabis and Aziza Bourouaha are meticulous craftswomen who prefer the traditional style. And they are not alone. In Sefrou, there is a great demand for these buttons, whereas Rachida's group doesn't make them at all.

The names for buttons are also completely different. The bildi is called semma in Sefrou, Rachida's "acorn" is Amina's "jasmine," and the "turban" is simply "chain" in Sefrou. These differences between the two towns, only one hundred miles apart, highlight the rich variations that exist in a country with myriad local craft traditions.

Top row: A shop where Rachida buys her thread; Fatima holding spools of thread before she plies it.
Center: Rachida beginning to form a classic jacquard button, starting with tubing to cut for the center.
Bottom row: Basic jacquard button and a necklace made with jacquard buttons.

One thing is universal: in every town famed for its artisanry, be it weaving, embroidery, or button making, the names for designs are based on objects they are said to resemble. What is unique about Khenifra is that the resemblance is astonishingly clear. The turban design looks like a turban, the large and flat *sidi* looks like a CD, and the *shaariya* like little noodles. When I mentioned that real acorns were longer than the button variety, Rachida was quick to say that her acorn buttons imitated the short Spanish acorn, not the long Moroccan one!

Despite her personal preferences, Rachida pays attention to popular fads. When she's making buttons for jellabas, she decorates them in her client's chosen colors. But when she's making jewelry, she uses the styles and colors she likes best, as do each of the association members. Most of the members do similar work, and if one of the women has invented a unique style, she'll teach it to the others.

They buy the metallic findings in Marrakesh; Khenifra is too small to carry such things. Some are real silver, but many are not—to make things affordable. Taught by Peace Corps volunteers, the women of Khenifra set their own prices, which vary. A necklace may cost $30 in the U.S. at the Santa Fe Folk Art Market, but only $15 in Fes or on the Anou website. The higher price covers the costs of going to Santa Fe: hotel, food, airfare, booth rental, and more. And they give discounts for large orders. Products are shipped to Rabat by the Moroccan post's version of priority mail, and then abroad by DHL, with which Anou has a special agreement.

Rachida has never created a new style of button, but she does use older designs in new ways. "A button that was originally designed for earrings, I use for necklaces. Sometimes I combine different colors when I ply the threads. Everyone has her own ideas. If I thought of something new, I'd show it to the other women. It shouldn't be just mine. We're a group, we share."

Yet in this association the money is not divided equally among its seventeen members. Each woman is paid according to the work she does. Rachida doesn't keep track of her earnings, which tend to be irregular. But as treasurer of the association she is certainly aware of payments made to members. Two weeks earlier, the group was paid for an unusually large order, and each woman received $105. Three weeks before that, each woman earned about $52. Rachida probably received the same amount.

Rachida spends her income on clothes, doctor's visits, glasses, the dentist, and on routine household expenses. Her father's salary covers food, electricity, basic supplies, and tutoring for the two

Buttons mixed with beads are shaped into a necklace.

children still attending school. Nevertheless, Rachida "can't stand by when my family needs something." In contrast, one of her brothers, who has a job as a guard in Fes, earns a regular paycheck, but he "doesn't help the family at all, not a penny! We give him bus fare to go home, plus he asks for $20 or $30 to take back with him." This is typical in Morocco, where men are pampered while the "weaker sex" is expected to help meet family needs—and does.

Rachida endures her erratic income because she sees other benefits to this craft. "If a woman is really expert at making buttons, people respect her. She'll be good at whatever she does."

"That's true," Fatima agrees. "If a girl knows a craft, a man will want to marry her. They'll say she's hadga, she'll know how to do embroidery, she'll keep house well. If she's really good at one thing, she'll be perfect in everything."

Rachida laughs. "Buttons are definitely one thing I know how to do. I didn't finish my studies so I don't have anything else. I could have been a seamstress, but buying fabric is expensive. I'd have to buy a machine, and that requires a lot of money, plus I'd need a place to keep it. Buttons are easier. I can sit down anywhere and make them. Besides, I get to travel and to meet a lot of people. Yes, I really enjoy my work."

Buttons are part of the traditional beauty of Morocco, a necessary adornment in constant demand. The association's newer line of costume jewelry has yet to find a similar niche with a similar demand. Sales at the Folk Art Market in Santa Fe are huge, but only one time a year, or alternate years.

Rachida's association has also sold through two shops that cater to tourists (Café Clock in Fes and Majorelle Gardens in Marrakesh) as well as two online sites: the shop of the International Folk Art Museum, in Santa Fe, and Anou. Another Peace Corps volunteer initiated these four commercial contacts on behalf of the group, and it is her outside help that forged their current marketing strategy. However, they have tried other outlets in Morocco.

Several years ago the women tried to establish relations with a store in the nearby village of Midelt, a popular tourist stop. After placing some jewelry there, they discovered that the manager took 50 percent of the sales price and that a number of pieces had disappeared. This experience, which is not uncommon for other artisans, discouraged the women from pursuing other markets in Morocco.

Overall, the Women's Crafts of Khenifra Association has been fairly successful at selling the women's products, and other women are eager to join. However, taking in new members has raised a few frustrations.

"They don't have enough patience when there's no income for a month or two," Rachida says. "We've gotten used to it, but they haven't. And they need a lot of training to learn to make the items we do."

"That's not all," Fatima complains. "We've been operating since 2008, and some still don't understand how an association works. They need training in that too. Illiterate women who haven't been to school just don't get it, even if you explain in Berber. And some can't write their names on the sales tags of their pieces. They can make the buttons, but they can't write."

Rachida cites some of the personal issues women face. "There are plenty of women who really want and need to work, and their skills are excellent. They just need people to work with." Fatima adds, "One woman's husband left her with a bunch of kids and she works in a pastry shop to earn a bit of bread. Another woman has no husband. We have two girls whose father died, several who have to help their families, and one whose husband doesn't work at all in the winter and she supports him.

"We want to work. We're not asking for handouts. We need literacy projects. We need places to sell. That's our main problem: marketing. We need good marketing and good clients. Our products are beautiful—everyone who sees them likes them—but we need to connect with major buyers."

Fatima adds, "Khenifra is small with no tourists, we don't know the Internet very well, don't know markets, don't know language, and the women aren't educated. That's the kind of assistance that someone could give us if they showed up." While they are doing well for a small rural women's group, they are ambitious: they would like to expand, to have clients in Europe and the Far East, and a steady flow of work.

Rachida and Fatima are competent young women who are doing their best to help their association members succeed. Because they did so well at the International Folk Art Market in 2014, they applied again, and after filling out volumes of forms in English, were accepted for 2016. Unfortunately, the U.S. Consulate would not grant Rachida a visa to visit the United States even though this would have been her second business trip. The women had already spent their own money on materials and produced a lot of jewelry in anticipation of selling it at the Santa Fe market and naturally were disappointed. Happily, a solution was found. The Peace Corps volunteer who started the group, Linda Zahava, agreed to attend the exhibition in Santa Fe and sell their products. She was delighted to help out, and they were thrilled that she could and would. Like a true business, the association agreed to pay for her airfare and hotel with funds set aside for Rachida's trip (though she didn't accept this offer). As Rachida said, "We aren't asking for handouts." But they wisely use all the assistance they can get.

Beads in several different styles.

FATIMA BENAYAD
STARS AND SCORPIONS

FES (*FESSI*) EMBROIDERY IS THE ICONIC STYLE of Morocco, used to decorate the finest household articles. Highly prized, Fes embroidery resembles cross-stitch but is much more complicated. For one thing, the embroidery is exactly the same on both sides, with no visible knots or rough places on the back. Although women use an embroidery hoop, they do not rely on patterns printed on the fabric to serve as a guide. Instead, they count the threads and use patterns they have memorized. The technique is extraordinarily difficult, and because the stitching is so delicate, embroiderers complain that it ruins their eyesight.

For centuries, Fes embroidery has been produced by women for women. During the nineteenth century, the upper class used silk thread to embroider fabrics that covered the banquettes and pillows in their parlors. Because the handwork is so time consuming, only a few drawloom weavers reproduce this kind of work for use on furniture today. Their work is not quite as fine as the hand embroidery, but it looks quite similar. But in the past fifty years, there's been a revival, and the heirloom pieces locked away in museums have been dusted off and given the attention they deserve. Once the province of the elite, costly embroidered linens are now an essential part of every bride's trousseau. Tablecloths, napkins, and decorative pillows are in wide demand. New mothers recycle their wedding sheet with matching pillowcases for their beds, using them after they've had a baby and when friends come to visit. Some will order a small piece of embroidered fabric to cover the cloth used to tie babies on their backs, although strollers and front-worn carriers are increasingly common.

Not surprisingly, change has affected the craft once again. The original impetus behind this great craft revival was not simply a matter of aesthetics. It was a concerted effort sponsored by the government to guarantee poor women an income. And it worked. Craft centers teaching embroidery sprang up everywhere, customers were lining up for embroidered table linens, and embroiderers' busy hands were taking in money. But just as this trend reached its pinnacle, along came the machines, able to copy beautiful designs for a fraction of the price.

The next few pages tell the tale.

ASHY, SOFT-SPOKEN WOMAN in her forties, Fatima Benayad hides a host of talents in her sewing basket. Fatima lives in Sidi Kacem Zawiya, a small town in the north central plains where I was based during my Peace Corps days in the 1960s and later lived while doing research. Over the years, I've watched the population mushroom with the influx of rural people searching for work. In the ebb and flow of life, Fatima's family has come to represent a certain stability, and they are my Moroccan family.

Although she is married and has two daughters, Fatima spends most of her time in her mother's house, the same house in which she was born. Fatima's husband is a housepainter who is often away, working in Tangier, and she appreciates the company of her mother and her former neighbors, who drop in and out all day.

When Fatima completed fifth grade, she left primary school and went directly to the local women's center where she learned

Opposite: Traditional Fes style, or fessi, embroidery embellishes the finest household items in Morocco.

to knit, sew, and do hand and machine embroidery. She immediately picked up "shadow" embroidery and by the age of fifteen had mastered the more difficult Fes style. "In a year you can learn everything. You just see something with your eyes, and you copy it."

The women's center hasn't changed much in the fifty years since I worked there except for the addition of machines that do embroidery in addition to the tabletop sewing machines. Yet many have learned to sew garments for their relatives and a few support their families by doing Fes embroidery. Fatima certainly used her embroidery skills to improve her life, both economically and creatively.

Fatima began by teaching the neighbor girls how to embroider in the Fes style. Her classes started with small designs and ended with the diamond-shaped "big nutmeg," a complex pattern that fills the center of a tablecloth. She didn't charge for the lessons because the neighbor girls are like her sisters.

Fatima does the Fes style mainly because it is in high demand and she can do the work at home. "People come and order it from us. I don't have to go wandering around, selling it. A woman knocks at the door and asks if you'll do some embroidery for her. The pay is a little low, but there isn't any other work here. At least you don't have to go to work as a maid in someone else's house. You're in your own home, taking care of your children, and you're embroidering. Machine embroidery pays better, and it's easier to do. With fessi, you have to count the threads and your eyes hurt. All the same, my brain learned fessi, and I've stuck with it."

Off and on, Fatima works on a piece she began when she got married more than ten years ago. "It's my bridal sheet. I like it and I can't part with it. My mother tells me to sell it, but I refuse. I made it with passion. The central design was hard to make, and all the work was complicated. When it's finished and washed, I'll spread it out like a bedspread and I'll really enjoy it."

Mostly Fatima makes tablecloths and decorative pillows to order. She likes creating designs for tablecloths and feels a sense of pride when people buy and enjoy them. She especially likes making pillows using "bag" fabric (a coarser weave) because the thicker thread is easier on the eyes.

Master embroiderer Fatima Benayad at her mother's home in Sidi Kacem Zawiya.

"I embroider pillows for the traditional salon and for modern couches. A woman comes to my house and says, 'Make something pretty.' The woman chooses the basic color of the cloth, but I choose the designs and their colors. Sometimes clients invite me to their home, and I advise them on the pillow colors. If the upholstery is maroon, I fill in the design with maroon thread; if it's green, I use green. I work based on the color. The client likes it and I like it too.

"I get the designs from my mind. I start thinking, 'This would look nice, that would look bad.' If something comes out looking ugly, I rip it out and do a different design. It's the same with the colors that fill in the designs. If the color doesn't look good, I'll rip it out. I figure the client won't like it either. I like to create pretty designs."

Fatima invents her own designs. Sometimes she looks through embroidery books or examines her friends' work for new ideas, but she usually expands and alters the size and adds them to designs of her own.

There is a system for putting each design in place. After measuring and folding the fabric, she puts a needle in the center of the tablecloth, which is where the design begins. Then she embroiders "chains," moving out from the center to the edges, and uses her outstretched palm to measure where the "sprinkle" designs will go. She marks their placement with a pen and later embroiders over the mark.

The designs, shown in the photo on page 140, have many names. The central diamond shape is a piece of nutmeg (*gouza*); the star (*nejma*) looks like a star and is placed between the points of the nutmeg. "Sprinkle" (*reshHa*) designs are scattered across the surface and stand alone. The razor design (*zizwara*), composed of elongated hexagons with yellow edges, runs in diagonal chains. Then there are the scorpion (*agreb*) and the "bicycle handlebars" (*geedun dyal bikala*). These curved blue lines run along the perpendicular or horizontal chain from the center.

As for her materials, Fatima buys the white fabric in the nearby town of Sidi Kacem but sometimes has to go to Meknes to find the "bag" fabric in special colors like blue, green, brown, beige, and navy. On her trips to Sidi Kacem, she also purchases top-quality DMC mercerized cotton embroidery floss imported from

France. The color doesn't run when the tablecloths are washed and bleached after meals containing saffron. For the "bag" fabric, Fatima uses acrylic yarn, which is thicker than embroidery floss and shows up better.

Once she has her fabric and thread, Fatima starts embroidering at 6:00 in the morning. She'll pause to do chores and make bread for lunch, which one of her daughters carries to and from the pub-

A section of Fatima's bridal sheet.

lic wood-fired oven, and then works through the afternoon and evening while watching TV. She used to embroider with her circle of friends, "to keep each other company. But now that I have my daughters, I work alone."

As she embroiders, she keeps track of the number of balls of thread she uses. This is her way of calculating her time and ultimately her sale price. One ball of good DMC thread costs about $5. The total amount of the thread tells her the cost of the finished product.

Since the client provides the fabric and thread, the final price represents Fatima's labor. As a fringe benefit, she gets to keep the leftover fabric, which is usually enough to make little napkins or hankies to sell. For a round tablecloth about six feet in diameter, she charges $8. During her most productive times, she may earn a dollar a day. In comparison, the standard wage for a manual laborer is $5 a day and for her husband, the housepainter, $15 or more a day—but he is not always working. Fatima would have to work for two weeks to earn that much.

In any case, Fatima thinks she makes more money by dealing directly with clients rather than going through a middlewoman, as many do. "I won't give my work to someone else to sell so she'll benefit from it," she insists. "I'd rather work for a customer who comes to my house and asks me to make a tablecloth. I'll make it for a high price and keep the money for myself." But those orders come in sporadically. "People who are always working get orders from middlewomen. Every week, or even every four days, they finish something. Me, no. Just once in a while I get an order, but when I do it's a good one. It's honest work; I make something beautiful, and they pay me well.

"I used to save and buy gold, I'd save and buy jellabas, I'd save and buy a fancy party outfit, get all dressed up, and go to weddings. It's necessary to look as good as everyone else." Now she spends her income on school expenses and treats for her two daughters.

"In the old days, it was obligatory for a girl to make something using Fes embroidery. If you didn't, you'd be seen as worthless. At marriage, you had to make little hankies and give them out to members of the bride's and the groom's family at the breakfast following the wedding night. Then they'd be happy; they'd say, 'The girl embroiders, she has a skill. She's hadga, a hard worker who does things well.' But now it's not that way. No, no. Today they look for a girl who's working and educated. She can come with a suitcase full of embroidery and no one will marry or accept her. A girl with a job is better than a girl who embroiders.

"We aren't benefitting from embroidery anymore. It's become like old stuff in museums, antique, ancient, something we used to do. Embroidering and getting good pay so we can support our children, that's gone. Or maybe I'm just worn out. I'd keep work-

Fatima's colorful neighborhood in Sidi Kacem Zawiya.

The nutmeg design for the center of a tablecloth, illustrating the different designs described on page 137.

ing, but there needs to be money in it. When I sell my embroidery for a good price, it's okay, but I don't want to work really hard on something and get paid a low price. In fact, my work does sell at a good price. But those middlemen who bring us orders give us a low price."

To illustrate her point, Fatima says that bridal sheets don't sell well now. They cost $200 to have made, but you can buy a bedspread for $50 and be done with it. The "counterfeit" machine-made Fes sheets, complete with long and square embroidered pillows, look pretty from a distance and cost only $20. Except for the very well off, most brides today buy the machine embroidered sheets. " I hope my daughters will end up with a good profession, like teacher, doctor, or architect, something where they can earn money to live well. We need to work to get what we want. My daughters need to succeed at their studies so they can get a good job with the government or with a company, God willing. They can earn much better money than for the handwork I do."

Early on, Fatima took charge of her life. When it was time for marriage, she had the opportunity to wed two cousins. One was from a nearby town and it didn't work out. The other was from a nearby village, and she flatly refused him. "I thought he'd take me to the country and have me live there, and I didn't want to live out in the boonies. To bake in an earth oven and live without indoor running water—no way." Her husband is the son of a neighbor, and the fact that she lives in town and can spend so much time with her mother while he travels has worked out well for her.

Fatima's choice in marriage is a sign of changing times. Her accommodating mother agreed to marry a neighbor her father chose for her, a man who had been in the French army and had a pension, but to whom she had never spoken. She did not dare defy her family. But Fatima could, and did, make her own choices, in her marriage and in her craft.

Fatima's passion for embroidery is undercut by economic realities. She is adamant about not working for a middlewoman and clear about her desires for her children. Although she takes enormous pleasure in the art of it, she sees Fes embroidery as a declining craft. She does not plan to teach her daughters embroidery.

ZINEBE BOUNOUARA
MIDDLEWOMAN

WHEN I MET ZINEBE BOUNOUARA, I was surprised to discover that this elegantly dressed young businesswoman who travels alone to Tangier to sell embroidery is from a rural village that offers few educational and career opportunities for women. But Morocco is full of surprises.

Her village of Ben Abdiya lies forty kilometers from the city of Meknes, in north central Morocco. The region's fertile plains are green with wheat, vegetables, and olive trees and red with wild poppies in the spring. Zinebe was born in a hospital twenty-nine years ago, about the time when women were choosing hospital births rather than home deliveries. Her husband is a guard at a gas station in Meknes and comes home every two weeks. They do not have children yet. Since it would not be proper for her to live alone, Zinebe lives with her husband's family, who runs a farm outside the village. This means that there is more than one woman to perform the many household chores.

After Zinebe finished primary school, she was unable to continue her studies. "When I moved to junior high in the bigger town, I had no place to live. There was no money to stay in town and no money for me to go back and forth from my village every day. So I dropped out and stayed home and learned embroidery from other village girls. What I saw, I copied. I only had to look at the designs and I could do them. When I was twelve, I began embroidering for money."

Zinebe is now an expert in embroidery and as a middlewoman. Her second career fills a great need. Most embroiderers depend on women like Zinebe who save them the trouble of getting orders and buying materials and, more importantly, make it possible for

The enterprising Zinebe Bounouara.

them to earn money while staying at home and caring for children.

Zinebe began selling for others three years ago. "I started out by making things for a woman who sold them. One day I asked her where she goes, and I began to go to the same places by myself." Zinebe went to Tangier, where she had family she could stay with. It took about two years to get into a comfortable routine. At first she made contacts through her family, but now each time she travels to the city, she ventures into a new neighborhood and just knocks on doors.

Zinebe makes and sells sheets and pillow covers, tablecloths and napkins, and baby cloths decorated with Fes embroidery. "It's a lot of work, but I like the designs. It's like a drawing. It takes time, but when it's finished, you know you've made something pretty."

A potential threat to Zinebe's craft and sales is the recent invention of machines that produce "Fes-style" embroidery. As

An embroidered pillow in process.

Fatima Benayad mentioned earlier, at first glance, the work looks the same as the original, but on closer inspection you can see the difference. The telltale sign is the back of the cloth, which is very unlike the front. But aside from quality, the real threat is the price. A hand-embroidered bridal sheet may cost $300 to $500, whereas a machine-made sheet sells for $80 to $120; the price for a handmade set of tablecloth and napkins runs about $100, but a machine-made set is available for as low as $40. Competition with manufactured articles is not a concern for Zinebe right now because she has enough clients who want custom-made pieces in their choice of designs and colors.

Zinebe chooses between two kinds of fabric: *la toile* ("canvas") and *xaysh* ("sackcloth"). The latter is a soft, stain-resistant acrylic that is easier to work on but is double the price. The sackcloth comes in many colors, though this is hardly a factor since white and off-white sell best. As for thread, she steers away from that

which is labeled DMC from France because in her markets, it might be counterfeit and the colors might run. Rather than take the risk, she buys a new polyester thread that comes in long groups of strands. Using one strand is usually sufficient, but two heighten the design. She buys her thread and fabric in the big stores in Meknes.

When she's not out selling, Zinebe embroiders all year, even during holidays and Ramadan. She works all day and up to 11:00 at night. "I'm always embroidering; I can't sit down without doing it."

Once a month, Zinebe makes the three-hour trip, by bus or train, to Tangier. "I take what I've made to my client, her friend will see it and want one, and next time I go, I'll take what she's ordered. Word spreads." Just to make sure, Zinebe knocks on neighbors' doors and shows them the finished product before she delivers it to her client. The direct approach works in her favor; shops are rarely interested and when they are, they pay less. A tablecloth and napkins sold to an individual might earn her a $20 profit, whereas a shop would bring her only $5. She's found it best to avoid them. If she didn't stay with her family in Tangier, her profits would barely cover expenses.

Zinebe's sale price depends on the time and effort she puts into a piece. Some embroidered tablecloths may take ten days, others a month. Beyond that, she takes into account the cost of fabric, thread, and transportation. If she's very busy, she may hire other embroiderers to help out, in which case she pays per item. Zinebe is one of the few artisans I've met who keeps a complete accounting of her costs.

Of course, the price she sets is subject to Morocco's intense bargaining culture. "They tell you it's pretty, you say a price, she tells you a price, back and forth until you agree. If she offers you a price that you don't lose money on, you sell. If she offers you a price that you'll lose money on, you leave."

Her estimated income as a middlewoman also has its ups and downs. Her total costs for a simple tablecloth and napkins that took fifteen days to make came to $30. "I'll get $15 to $20 profit if I just want to get rid of it. If I ask a higher price, I can probably make $50 to $60 for the set."

Examples of traditional fessi embroidery on pillows and sheets.

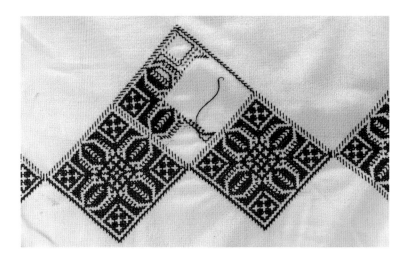

Compare this to Fatima Benayad, who earned $8 for a round tablecloth with a complicated pattern that took her two weeks to embroider. Zinebe says she paid $10 for the plainer work. Fatima's notion that she would earn less from a middlewoman has no basis; in fact, she would have more steady work and earn about the same per tablecloth. True, the middlewoman earns up to three times more than the embroiderer. But Fatima would not earn less if she sold through a middlewoman.

Zinebe's contribution to the family income is substantial. Her husband earns $150 a month as a guard at a gas station. In a good month, Zinebe can sell ten tablecloths and earn the same amount. Since she lives on his parents' farm, the savings from that, though hard to determine, is rightly part of the total. In short, Zinebe's work is a tremendous help.

Although she enjoys embroidery work and selling, Zinebe says neither is easy. "Traveling around is hard. And embroidery is hard. It can take me a whole day to make one napkin. The tablecloth took me a month. What I'd like is for people to send me orders for the kind of embroidery they want, and I'd make it and sell it to them without having to keep traveling far away and looking for the work."

Left: A bridal sheet with embroidery along the top edge. See detail on page 143.
Below: Zinebe spent a day embroidering one of these napkins and a month on the matching tablecloth.

THE "PERSISTENT ONES"

THE ARTISANS PRESENTED IN THIS BOOK have created fulfilling lives for themselves and their families through strength, determination, and creativity. The seven members of the **Assabirate Cooperative** in Marrakesh are no exception, even though, as women with disabilities, they face exceptional challenges.

Being disabled in Morocco is difficult for both women and men. Until recently, few public places were accessible, wheelchairs were scarce, and most people with disabilities were confined to their homes. Responding to these needs, King Mohammed VI has made it a priority to assist those who are poor or have disabilities by providing wheelchairs, crutches, and various government services. Nevertheless, those in wheelchairs cannot board buses or maneuver in the streets. And none of the established services begin to address the economic side of the problem. It is difficult for anyone in the country to find a job, much less for a person with disabilities to do so. Jobs are less essential for women, but having a disability limits their options for marriage as well as their ability to support themselves and achieve independence.

The women of the Assabirate Cooperative have surmounted these issues. When I first met them several years ago, I was struck by their warmth, pride, pragmatism, and humor. They have been working together for twenty years, became a cooperative in 2004, and by now are longtime friends. They remind me of neighborhood girls who have time to hang out together, chat about anything and everything, and not be drawn away by family duties. Last time we visited, they were teasing one of the members about her upcoming wedding, everyone speaking at once, and embroidering the tablecloths and sheets for her trousseau. They're all working, creating beautiful embroidery in different styles, and earning an income.

The name *Assabirate* is difficult to translate. In one sense it means patient, putting up with problems. But the word is more nuanced than that. The Arabic word *sber* refers to one of the most valued human traits in Islam: to endure in difficult situations—and not complain about it. And so alternate translations could be endurance, persistence, forbearance, resilience, hardiness, or passive resistance. I have chosen "persistent" to convey the essence of this close-knit group.

We met in their workplace, a spare but comfortable space with three small rooms in a nondescript government-owned building located in a residential neighborhood of Marrakesh. One room is furnished with traditional banquettes where the women sit together and embroider, the second room is equipped with sewing machines and supplies, and the third is set up as a salesroom, open by appointment. They used to have a place in the old medina, which was much easier for clients to find, but they had to move. This building is so hidden away that there is no walk-in traffic. On the plus side, the government gave them this spot as part of the initiative for individuals with disabilities, and although the women must pay utilities, the rent is free. Despite the undistinguished location, the women have made it a cozy place to work and to showcase the clothing and linens they embroider.

Most of the women were born in southern Morocco and moved to the city with their parents when they were young. They are now in their late thirties and forties, and only Nadia Mahjoubi is married. Some went to primary and secondary school, others attended adult literacy classes. The highest educational level is tenth grade.

The seven women met in a training program for people with

disabilities offered by the Hassan the Second Foundation in Marrakesh. The trainees were given materials, learned manual skills, and had their finished products sold by the foundation. The women were each paid a fixed sum of $65 a month, but that amount was too low for the women to live on. They began working together in 1994 while still at the Foundation, moved to their current workshop in 2000, and formed an official cooperative in 2004.

Left to Right: Nadia, Khadija, Fatima, and Zohra of the Assabirate Cooperative.

and earning money. Her specialty is Fes embroidery, which she calls *belhseb*, "by counting," since making the designs involves counting threads. In addition, she does machine embroidery and crochet.

Fatima Lakhtiri also studied at a women's center and was showing her gift for Fes embroidery at age fifteen. She is also proficient in the Rabat style, which uses satin stitch. Another woman learned the Fes style from girlfriends when she was eighteen. And she didn't do it for money; no, she was just "crazy about it."

Several members acquired their skills at the foundation when they were already in their twenties. It took Fatima Laksais, the co-op president, two or three years to master the craft. More typically, Fatiha El Wiskili learned embroidery when she was twelve. She started at a women's center, and within a month was getting orders

All the women are expert now, and each has a favorite style. While Samira Benayad (page 110) does satin stitch machine embroidery on women's party robes, the women in the cooperative use Fes embroidery on clothing, a creative step that I have not seen anywhere else. Fatima Laksais prefers the Rabat style because of its

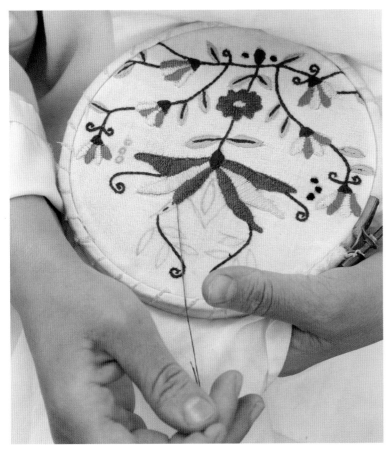

opment (INDH), another of the king's initiatives to assist the poor, donated the machines. Yet Zohra prefers the more difficult work of hand embroidering in the Fes style.

It's not surprising, then, that among the co-op's products, Fes embroidery is the outstanding style. Fatiha likes it "because it's always in demand and few know how to do it. To make both sides the same, hardly anyone wants to do that. It takes patience and being in the right mood. You have to count the threads, count and count. This younger generation, they aren't interested. They want to finish everything quickly."

The other skill that almost all of the women have is making the randa needle-woven trim, which joins the fabric at the fronts of women's jellabas and qaftans. They also make *tedris*, a needle-woven trim to edge sleeves. The wide main trim (*sfifa*) was originally made and applied to the fabric by men, but women have been making this complex trim for several generations.

The Persistent Ones are always working together on something.

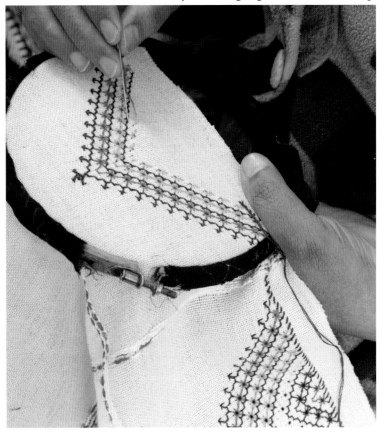

Above: Fatima, who prefers the Rabat style, stitches yellow and orange flowers to resemble the jemra blossoms sometimes used for natural dye. She draws the design in pencil before she embroiders, although not everyone does.
Right: Zohra counts the threads in her Fes style embroidery.

beautiful colors and varied designs. Nadia also prefers the Rabat style, especially for embroidering scarves. The voluble Khadija likes "everything": Fes and Rabat styles of embroidery and making *randa* (needle-woven) trim.

Fatima draws the design in pencil before she embroiders. Others keep the design in mind after having used it several times. Where do they get their designs? "You imagine them," Khadija says. "Or you might see something in a book or magazine, on TV, or on a fancy qaftan and draw it so you can copy it later."

Zohra Maamar and Atiqa Nkhili often embroider their pieces on a sewing machine. The National Initiative for Human Devel-

They come in daily and work from 10:00 a.m. to 7:00 p.m. No one works at home, where they have household chores. They do take Sundays off and the full month of August. This schedule, common in France, has been widely adopted in Morocco.

In their work, thread is the most important material. For the Fes style, they use DMC thread and for Rabat style, DMC and shiny sabra, which is made from rayon. For the randa trim they use either regular sabra, which consists of a single strand, or *sbaniya,* which has several strands twisted together. The women think the regular is prettier because of the way it shimmers, but each chooses the thread she prefers.

As an independent cooperative, The Persistent Ones set the prices for their products. Other co-ops may sell similar pieces at higher prices, but these women prefer to be competitive. They take into account the price of fabric, thread, and their labor. The more embroidery, the more expensive the item.

Their major sales outlets are expositions sponsored by the Ministry of Handicrafts. These fairs are usually held in Morocco, but sometimes abroad. In 2014, Fatima, the co-op president, was sent to Ghana with an array of embroidered garments and linens. Sales were poor, mainly because Ghanians were unfamiliar with the craft, but Fatima did make some important contacts. At the twice-yearly expositions in Morocco, each lasting twenty days, they sell well and also receive custom orders from people who admire their excellent work. Occasionally, tourists visit their shop and buy.

Like a true cooperative, they share their income. Each month, they tally sales, deduct the price of materials as well as co-op expenses such as phone and utilities, and calculate their profit. At the end of each month, they split the profit equally, no matter who did how much work. "Shared work, shared profit," the president says. These monthly profits range from $40 to $95 per person. In a recent month, each earned about $50. Sometimes the women have to chip in their own money to cover the phone bill and then repay themselves the following month. Yet they are not discouraged. They have been together a long time, have been patient, and have endured. At least they are earning an income, something not all Moroccans are able to do.

Most of the women live with their families. To live alone would be cost prohibitive and break societal rules. Although they earn very little, they still help their families with expenses and can afford to make lunch together at work.

When they thought about the impact of embroidery on their lives, they considered the group as a whole. "If we get an order, it enhances our reputation. Everyone's reputation benefits with good work."

Although the women love embroidery, they are not optimistic about its future:

"The majority of people who care about traditional handicrafts are foreigners. Those are our clients, and they're the only ones who value our work."

"Nowadays the skill isn't there anymore. Someone who is willing to sit patiently, work little by little, and get paid a little money is rare. This generation wants things fast and they want money right away. It's a problem. Also, there's no pension or health insurance so people don't want to do it; they have nothing after long years of work. It's just us, people a little older. When we die, it will be gone."

"Me, it's my eyes. See these glasses? The doctor said, 'Don't keep on with this work. Stop!' But it's not possible to stop. What am I going to do? I got glasses. There's no other option. We don't have the educational level to work in government or in an office. We can't even do cleaning. There's no alternative."

"That's why we named the cooperative Assabirate, The Persistent Ones, The Enduring Ones."

"We had a lot of problems when we began. We didn't find funds to buy fabric, we didn't have money to buy thread, we'd borrow from our parents, we needed money for transport."

"But if we had split up, each in her own house, our parents would still be supporting us just so we could eat and drink. But we wanted to make our future, we didn't want to be asking for handouts from our parents or our families."

"We were persistent. If we hadn't hung in there, overcome obstacles, we would not have gotten to where we are today, been able to form a co-op and still be together."

THE FUTURE

WHEN ARTISANS TAKE THE TIME to look up from their looms, embroidery hoops, and needles and cast their eyes to the future, their view of traditional crafts is shaped not so much by dedication or money but by the society around them. A few are certain that weaving, button making, and embroidery will endure for as long as the winds sweep through the olive groves. Most are wary of the cultural pressures blowing in from other parts of the world.

Habiba Lrhachi, like other young working women living in Tangier, has neither the time nor the living space to work at the loom. If and when she does, her exposure to new ideas leads to imaginative, though nontraditional, styles of weaving.

Passing on traditional skills to young people is the tried and true way to guarantee the survival of a craft, yet this transference is now hampered by a growing generation gap. When Kheira Ilahiane tried to start an association where experienced weavers would instruct young women, the project foundered, largely because the teenagers weren't interested in "old-fashioned" skills. Instead, they wanted to learn to knit and embroider on machines.

Another problem with Kheira's project was that the older women wanted to be paid to teach, rather than sharing their skills with the community as they would have in the past. The expansion of a cash economy with paid daily labor competes with pursuit of traditional skills. As Fatima Fdil in Ben Smim said, "It used to be that a woman would finish a rug every four or five days and then start another. Now they go off and work in agriculture, planting onions or squash and weeding the government's wheat fields." They need the immediate income.

Increased education, for which so many have struggled, can be a double-edged sword. "The young are finished," Fatima Lrhachi told me. "Education took them. They sit at the PC all day. Are they going to card wool?"

The members of the Assabirate Cooperative were equally skeptical about the future of Fes embroidery. Young women lacked the patience, they said. "This generation wants things fast and they want money right away . . . When we die, it's gone."

Many women expressed their doubts about whether weaving can compete with manufactured products. Cheaper, machine-made rugs in synthetic fabrics are glutting the markets, along with machine-embroidered table linens. These are the items most customers can afford. As the women in the Assabirate Cooperative point out, foreigners, rather than native buyers, value their handwork. Only the button makers are free of worries of being replaced, yet their craft keeps them just above subsistence level. But they, too, are concerned about its being carried on by the young. Girls don't like to work at home; they would rather work outside where they can meet boys. Yet rural girls and women still make buttons, because they have no other kind of paying work.

Most women derive enormous satisfaction from their craft and are happy to work at home where they can take care of their children. Yet a surprising number must provide financial support for their families. Those women who join successful cooperatives and associations enjoy greater self-esteem and camaraderie, but they will never reap material benefits such as health insurance or pensions.

Marketing is the most critical issue facing independent artisans and groups. The Moroccan government sponsors local and national craft exhibitions to address this problem; the Assabirate

Fatima El Mennouny and Fatima Id Rahou hold a rug being photographed for the Anou website.

embroiderers attend them, but they are held only once or twice a year, not enough for sustainable sales.

To help solve this problem, in 2001 I used my website, www.marrakeshexpress.org, to promote the work of women in two villages. Women could market to the whole world and avoid a middleman taking most of the profit (I worked pro bono). I posted photographs of the rugs with a description, the size and price, and a photo of the weaver with a brief biography including number of children and how she would use the money. This worked well—though it was easier said than done. To make it sustainable, I tried to find a Moroccan woman replacement with computer skills and English; she would make a commission on each rug. Although some women had the qualifications, none wanted to take it over. But in 2015, the women were able to join Anou.

As Kenza Oulaghda explains, the online site Anou offers a promising alternative to the usual, often exploitative, avenues of selling. "If the women hadn't found some improvement, they wouldn't have kept weaving; a woman needs some kind of motivation."

ANOU ("THE WELL" IN TAMAZIGHT) was designed to meet the problems many artisans face in trying to market their products. Founded by Peace Corps volunteer Dan Driscoll in 2012 and now affiliated with the Ministry of Handicrafts as a national cooperative, this successful project does away with middlemen and encourages craftspeople throughout Morocco to display and sell their work through their online site. The crafts sold on the site are remarkably diverse and include button necklaces and earrings produced by the Women's Crafts of Khenifra Association, described by Rachida Ousbigh, rugs woven by the Tithrite Association, under the leadership of Kenza Oulaghda, and rugs by the Timnay Association in the village of N'kob, home of several weavers here: Aicha Seqqat, Ijja Id Ali Boufkir, Jamila Samaa, Anaya Seqqat, Fatima El Mennouny, Fatima Id Rahou, Kebira Aglaou, and Fadma Buhassi.

Anou has a phone app that allows artisans connected to Anou to market their products directly to consumers anywhere in the world. Anou works with cooperatives or associations, rather than individuals, and trains them to photograph, price, and post their products online using a smartphone app designed for illiterate users. Anou maintains the website in English and handles international shipping and money transfer. The income goes directly to the artisan's postal savings account. Seventeen percent of the sale price covers Anou's costs. This amount and shipping are added to the artisans' asking prices so they are not out any money.

In addition to its high-tech approach, Anou is innovative in other ways. For one thing, it is artisan-led. Currently there are four national leaders, two men and two women, who work with more than 500 artisans. Kenza Oulaghda of the Tithrite Association is one of them.

"We have a personal tie with the client. Through the Internet, we talk about our products and our work. Our rugs are made in our town and photographed in our town, and so people can learn about our craft, watch the woman as she weaves, and see all the stages it goes through.

"Sometimes buyers in the market say, 'That rug isn't so special. It's not worth the price.' But they don't understand all the steps and how much time women spent on it. The women wash the wool, card, and spin it before they sit down to weave. That's done with all our traditional wool items. It doesn't just happen. There's a lot of work and bother before it gets to the client.

"Another good thing about Anou is that there's no middlemen, who take 50 or 60 or 70 percent. Anou is fighting things like that. Now we can make decent earnings, and the shipping is included. That's what's encouraged us." Since joining Anou in 2013, Kenza's association had sold more than sixty rugs online by 2016.

Kenza admits that, like many artisans, she knew nothing about the Internet and was "afraid of computers." But she's learned quickly. As for other association members, "only a few put their things online themselves, but that's what I'm working on. Any woman can learn. There are symbols to put things online. With the symbols, she doesn't need to be educated or know how to read or know English. I'm also showing them how to take photos. It would be easy for them all to market their products."

Anou's founder believes that crafts should evolve, and toward that end, the organization provides training workshops in design,

Jamila Samaa is learning how to take photographs suitable for the website from artisan leader Mustafa Chaoui.

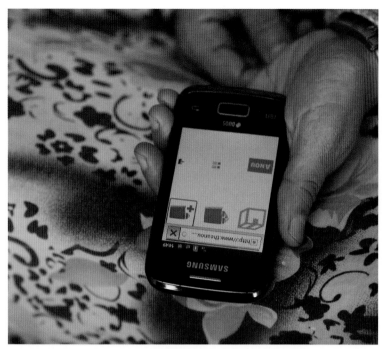

Kenza demonstrates how she uses her cell phone to upload photos to sell her rugs through the Internet.

creativity, and production values. Again, Kenza was one of the artisan leaders who participated in the Common Threads Project, sponsored by Anou and the British Council. During the one-week workshop, Kenza and the others acquired "new design tools that will enable artisans to create designs inspired by their personal stories, community, and craft."

When Kenza returned to her village, she wove a rug based on her new ideas. She also encouraged the weavers to try these ideas, which led to major changes in her association's rug designs: greater planning—as well as innovation.

New Designs

Fdila Azreg resolves her need for a steady income by working for a private European company that hires the women in her village to weave rugs. In time, the company's modern designs may affect the traditional style of Amassine. Because no culture can afford to remain static, Anou also encourages women to evolve and to try new styles. The difference is that the European company imposes designs and colors and Anou encourages individual creativity.

Strength and Spirit: The Way Forward

All of these complex questions hinge on the choice between tradition and change. The future of traditional crafts is threatened by factors such as widespread education, an expanding cash economy, and a consumer culture that provides inexpensive manufactured alternatives to many handmade items. It may blossom through innovative design and Internet marketing.

As they have demonstrated in their stories, Moroccan artisans are very capable of making choices for themselves. Think about Amina Yabis, the button maker who ran for office in 1994, not to win but to show local women that it could be done. Or Kheira Ilahiane, who ran for office to win in 2009 and did win, and says, "If we wait for men to give us our rights, they won't. Thank God that the king gave us our rights. And praise God that we're going to go further." Or Aicha Duha, who supports four people as a middlewoman selling rugs in a male domain. Or the weaver Fadma Wadal, a little girl stealing wool off sheep she was herding and hiding it in a graveyard at night, so she could learn to spin and weave. And later getting tattooed, although she knew her husband wouldn't like it. Or Samira Benayad, the seamstress and teacher who met her husband on the Internet. Do they seem like the stereotypical passive, submissive Muslim women to you?

While all of the women here have made choices influencing their own lives, some are reaching farther, to expand the choices of other women. Kheira says so emphatically above, and it's working: after she was in a documentary on TV, other local women were inspired and asked her how to run for office, and others marched to the governor's office to protest a decision. Habiba Lrhachi felt the important things she'd done in her life were to teach women to read, and to increase their income by selling their rugs on the Internet. Amina Yabis established cooperatives and gave how-to classes to give women a chance to earn more. Kenza Oulaghda is helping women around Morocco earn more by being an artisan leader with Anou and is also helping her fellow villagers by having local projects sponsored by the weavers' association.

With their usual wisdom, strength, and humor, the women of Morocco will decide their future.

A SELECTED GLOSSARY OF ARABIC AND BERBER TERMS

A note on the transcription of Arabic and Tamazight or Tashelhit (Berber) words: Although there are standard systems, most would be too esoteric for the readability of a book like this. I have written most words as I hear them, and they may sometimes vary. The Arabic letter *ain* has no transliteration in English and is represented as 3, which can be roughly pronounced as ah.

Key: Words in gold are Berber; those in black are Arabic. Red words are the same in both languages.

abaya A long black cloth draped over a woman's head and body but not face in Iran

aghlaf A long flatwoven bag with a shoulder strap, traditionally used by Anti-Atlas men

ago Soot, used in natural dyes in the Anti-Atlas

agreb "Scorpion," a design in Fes embroidery

aheddoun A woman's cape in the Middle Atlas, also called *tehendirt*, or *hendira* in Arabic; a simple man's cape in the Anti-Atlas

ahendir A woman's cape in southeastern Morocco, also called *tebban* or *hendira*

ahidour Rugs containing flatweave and twining in the Anti-Atlas (can be only black and white, or can contain colored patterns in the flatweave)

akhnif Man's cape woven to shape, some decorated with fine symbols, also used for flatweave rugs with embroidery-like decoration, in the Anti-Atlas

akhnif "Picture" rug with squares containing different designs, sometimes separated by a border in pile, or having some squares in pile; some artisans in N'kob call these rugs *akhnif* or *bu tilwah*

alkhossa Button style meaning "fountain"

Amazigh, Imazighren "Free man/men," the Tamazight name for Berbers

Arab Middle Atlas rug design of a diamond shape outlined in small diamonds

aska Beater to secure weft in rugs in the Middle Atlas; also called *haska*

asTa lman "Congratulations on the loom/weaving": reply to warp winding prayer in southeastern Morocco

asTa Weaving and loom in the Anti-Atlas

aznag, aznar A plainweave man's cape in the Anti-Atlas woven as a rectangle and cut to shape

a3ref Thicker weft yarn in southeastern Morocco, used in men's robes

3abana, 3aban pl Anti-Atlas blankets, also finely woven for a bride to wear going to her new home and to wrap dead people in on the way to the cemetery (but not buried with them). Blankets in southeastern Morocco.

3adem "Bone" or forearm, used to measure rugs. They say two spread palms equal one "bone," which is about 45 or 50 cm. Also used for a clan or subgroup in a tribe.

3amara Decorative trim on a *jellaba* or *qaftan;* also a bunch of 40 buttons used as part of that trim

3amer "Full" Middle Atlas flatweave with an overall geometric design and often sequins

3aqeda "Knot," used by a few in the Anti-Atlas to refer to knotted or pile rug

3aroud Weft yarn in Tamazight in southeastern Morocco, also *jerray* there

3azara "The bachelors" are warp threads outside the heddle loops in southeastern Morocco

belhseb "By counting," a term used for Fes embroidery

beloTa "Acorn," a style of jellaba button in Khenifra, with two colors of thread; called *jasmine* in Sefrou

benwar Warm bathrobe worn over women's winter clothing, from French *peignoir*

bettaniya, bettaniyat pl Blanket

bildi "Traditional," sometimes describes natural dyes. For buttons, it's the name of the "original" one in Khenifra, a style called **summa** in Sefrou

bimzghran A design of a star shape inside a hexagon; *imzghran* means ear

bismillah, tukulna ȝala allah "In God's name, we rely on God;" said when anchoring a loom in the Middle Atlas

boucherwite Rag rug, usually knotted rather than flatweave, made of rags bought at the market or of unraveled yarn from there or old family clothing

boushniqa A button style in Sefrou meaning dried flowers of Queen Anne's lace

bshim Weft yarn in Arabic; **jerray** or **ȝaroud** in Tamazight in southeastern Morocco

bstilla A button style named for a large, elaborate pastry and chicken dish

bu idraran The mountain one, a flatwoven rug from the Anti-Atlas consisting of many varied small designs in one piece, often curved so they resemble mountains, or they may resemble the maps (*kharitat*) women see in their children's school books

bu laqwas Anti-Atlas rug design of rectangular "arches"

bu tilwah Anti-Atlas "picture" rug with squares containing different designs, sometimes separated by a border in pile, though some artisans in N'kob just call these rugs **akhnif** and one calls them **azzugagh.**

chedwi Anti-Atlas flatweave rug that uses the technique of twining in black and white, rarely brown and white

dama "Squares," a style of Anti-Atlas rug with a lattice of squares outlined in smaller squares. Dama is also the name for the game of checkers.

dbagh A plant used by tanners, which made mauve, called "neck of the pigeon" in Ait Hamza

debbagh dyal korij Bark of the live oak, used to make brown dye in the Middle Atlas

defina A sheer overlayer for a *qaftan*

dellaha A button style in Sefrou meaning "watermelon"

djej "Chicken," Anti-Atlas rug motif that looks like a chicken

DMC Pronounced deem-see: imported cotton thread used for Fes embroidery

doum Palmetto grass, used to make Middle Atlas floor mats

dyal fitla One type of thread used for Fes embroidery; comes in strands and is sold by weight, probably polyester

dzza A fleece from a sheep

fessi "From Fes," the name of the embroidery style typical of Fes which is the iconic style of Morocco. It is also called **belhseb** or "by counting" and resembles counted cross-stitch, but is the same on both sides.

fikroun "Turtle," Middle Atlas rug motif resembling a turtle

frash "Furniture" for the home, which often consisted of blankets and rugs in the Middle Atlas and southeastern Morocco, where blankets are also called **ȝaban**, as they are in the Anti-Atlas

fuwa Red dye from madder root

fuwa "Crazy," an extra warp thread that doesn't fit into the alternating "householders" and "bachelors" warp threads, in southeastern Morocco

geedun dyal bikala "Bicycle handlebars," a design in Fes embroidery; words are Arabized French.

gholala A design like a chain stitch in embroidery, woven along the edges of a rug or bread cloth, used to protect against the evil eye, in southeastern Morocco

glaoui An Anti-Atlas rug style containing pile, twining, and flatweave

gouza kbira "Big nutmeg," a diamond shape in Fes embroidery for the center of a tablecloth

haddun Small and finely woven women's capes in the Middle Atlas

haik A long cloth women wore as outdoor covering before they began wearing jellabas

hanbel, hnabel pl Flatweave rugs in the Middle Atlas, sometimes called **kilim** by dealers, but they are not woven in **kilim** style with slits between colors

haska Beater to secure weft in rugs in the Middle Atlas; also called **aska**

hatif Middle Atlas rug design of triangles made up of triangles

hayk b mouzoun A woman's cape decorated with sequins in the Anti-Atlas

hebba "Seed," white yarn with bumps or "seeds" in it

hebil "Crazy," an extra warp thread that doesn't fit into the alternating "householders" and "bachelors" warp threads

hemel, hemoul pl Anti-Atlas simple striped flatweaves used to cover the floor *hendira, hendirat* pl Women's large capes in the Middle Atlas, often decorated with sequins, also called *tehendirt* or *ahaddoun* in Tamazight. *Hendira* is also used in southeastern Morocco, where they are also called *tebban* or *ahendir.*

henna Leaves from Lawsonia spp. used to color hair and also for dyeing rug wool in the Middle and Anti-Atlas; produces a red-brown or orange

hrir Silk; sometimes also used for rayon. No silk is produced in Morocco now.

hrir asili "Original silk," refers to good quality rayon thread used to make buttons; it won't run or fade

hrir mzawwer "Counterfeit silk," poor quality rayon thread for buttons

hsira Mat made in the Middle Atlas of palmetto grass

hzam A belt for a man or woman; used to be handwoven

iboli Anti-Atlas knotted rugs

iklan "Design," used for an older Anti-Atlas design, recently popular again, which is the same on both sides of the piece; may be another name for *teereera*. Also used to describe an Anti-Atlas flatwoven rug with black and white twining (*chedwi*) and colored *teereera* designs.

imeDliy Middle Atlas flatweave with an overall geometric design and often sequins; called *3amer* or full [of design] in Arabic

imighrz Middle Atlas rug design of facing zigzag lines

imizdareen A design of a diamond with extensions around it in N'kob. It means "little feet" in shilHa. The same design is called *tidareen* or "feet" in nearby Amassine.

inzadn Goat hair, in southeastern Morocco; must be mixed with wool to weave

ishkjid Finely woven tops of old Anti-Atlas boots that were attached to leather soles

isifen The especially nice wool that is used to make warp in southeastern Morocco; called *nserita* in Berber; sometimes combined with goat hair for strength

isigagen Boards that will be mounted at the bottom and top of the loom with the warp

izzalayn Anti-Atlas rug design of a small spot, "bead," or "jewel"

jacquard or jakar a style of needle-woven button, the basis for most others according to Rachida in Khenifra.

jebbad A "puller," used to maintain tension so the edges of rugs are even

jellaba Long outer garment with a hood, worn by both men and women

jerray Weft yarn in Tamazight in southeastern Morocco, also *3aroud* there

jrana "Frog," a Middle Atlas rug motif

kabel A thin handmade band of rayon that's used to cover seams and also for decoration on traditional clothing

kala The forearm, used to measure rugs in southeastern Morocco. They say two spread palms equal one forearm, about 45 or 50 cm.

ka3ba Finger joints, used to measure the width of stripes on women's capes, about 2 cm

kbibat Stitches in both Fes and Rabat embroidery resembling domes

kharita "Map," a flatwoven rug from the Anti-Atlas consisting of many varied small designs in one piece, which may

resemble the maps (*kharitat*) women see in their children's school books. Often curved so they resemble mountains, or *bu idraran*, in Berber.

kilims What Westerners call flatweave rugs, but those in Morocco do not have slits between color changes

la toile Fabric traditionally used for Fes embroidery. Although it means canvas in French, it is not that heavy or dense

lawat Fabric waste used to stuff banquette pillows and cushions; wool was used in the past

leHemel Black and white flatwoven pieces, used as rugs or to carry people to their graves but not for burial; same term in Amassine and N'kob in Anti-Atlas

lfrayza "Strawberry," a style of jellaba button in Khenifra that resembles a strawberry

lhakaka "Scrubber," a style of jellaba button in Khenifra with a rough surface

lizar A long cloth wound around a woman's body, used in place of the outer robe or *jellaba* in the past. Also a Middle Atlas bride's dress in the past.

lkhossa "Fountain," a style of jellaba button in Khenifra that resembles a fountain with a rim of different colored thread on one end

medina "City," the older, traditional part of a Moroccan city.

mendil Loosely woven red wool cloth used to cover bread as it is rising, in southeastern Morocco and the Anti-Atlas, sometimes decorated with some tie dyeing

menjel "Scythe," Middle Atlas rug motif like a zigzag

mensej An upright loom, the style women use for weaving

menshar "Saw," Middle Atlas rug motif of a toothed zigzag

mersha Middle Atlas rug design of a diamond outlined by triangles

meshiawrat Little embroidered hankies made by bride for both families (the Moroccan Arabic diminutive plural rendering of the French *mouchoir*)

mesht Handled combs with long teeth to process wool

meswak Walnut bark, used as a dye in southeastern Morocco and other areas

metdarin, or **meteedareen** Anti-Atlas rug design of a diamond with little lines going out from it, "little feet" or "toes." Also called *mulat rejlin*, the one with many feet or toes. Important element in borders.

metquna Tightly woven for rugs, well made for clothing

mexedda, mexedd Decorated woven pillow(s)

mezuwweq "Decorated," name of Middle Atlas flatweave rugs with alternating plain and decorated stripes

midra Metal beater used to pound down rows of weft in the Middle Atlas and southeastern Morocco

milhaf A long, gauzy cloth that covers the head and body but not the face, worn by women in far southern Morocco and Mauretania, often tie dyed in bright colors

mishmashi "Apricot," the name for the gold color that is widely used in Anti-Atlas pile rugs

mnawel Boards with warp attached that are mounted at the bottom and top of the loom

mramma Embroidery hoop, also used for the complex drawloom, and for a regular upright loom in southeastern Morocco

mwalin dar "Householders"; threads inside a heddle loop, so they have a "house," in southeastern Morocco

mwayen "Dishes, tools," used for the equipment used to weave

nadi or **nadi niswi** "Club/women's club," used in Morocco for government women's centers where they learn crafts

nejma "Star," a motif resembling a star in Fes embroidery

nilj Indigo, used to make some blue dye; best with addition of henna leaves, dates, and coal

niqab Full body covering worn by women in Yemen, with a narrow slit for the eyes.

niyyeru To tie the thread heddles onto the warp in southeastern Morocco; it plants the soul in the loom

nqiya "Clean"; a woman should be ritually clean when winding a warp

nserita The especially nice wool that is used to make warp in southeastern Morocco; called *isifen* in the Tamazight dialect of Berber there

nuwwar shems A button style meaning "sunflower"

orf Tribal law, especially concerning land and water and tribal disputes, still functioning in some rural parts of Morocco, as it is in the southeast in this book. It's different from national law, which is also practiced; *orf* sometimes takes precedence.

oushfoud Prickly broom flowers used to make yellow dye in the Anti-Atlas

outad dyal seddiya Stake in the ground for each end of winding the warp

pyjama Loose one- or two-piece outfit worn at home

qaftan, qfaten pl Long woman's party gown

qenn-rezm Middle Atlas rug design called shut-release

qershel Wool cards, also to card wool

qima The value of something

qsar, qsur pl Large fortified adobe home housing several families; sometimes a whole walled village, found mainly in southern Morocco

qsher Apple tree bark used to make yellow-gold dye in the Anti-Atlas

qsher roman Rind of pomegranate, used to make dye in the Middle Atlas

randa Needle-woven trim that can join fabric at the front of women's robes

reHal A nomad, who moves with his herds of sheep in the Middle Atlas

reshHa The "sprinkle" of designs on a Fes embroidered tablecloth; they vary from one to another

reshma General term for "designs," used in embroidery

rezza "Turban," a button style

ruH "Soul"; both people and rugs have them, located in the rug's shed

sabra Rayon thread and the name of a local aloe plant. Some sabra thread is said to be made from the aloe, sometimes called "cactus silk," but it's uncommon and of poor quality. Rayon is used to make needle-woven buttons and randa trim on garments.

sahel w xfif A prayer for women winding a warp in southeastern Morocco: "Light and easy," so the work will be that way

sbaniya Rayon *sabra* thread that has several strands plied or twisted together, used for *randa* trim

sba3iya Middle Atlas rug design called lion footprint

sber To endure in difficult situations, AND not to complain about it; to be patient or persistent

sda Warp

sebaniya A satin scarf worn by a Middle Atlas bride, their version of a wedding veil

sedd To dress a loom or wind a warp, also to start a rug

sedd-tleq "Shut-release," a Middle Atlas rug design

semma The original button style of Sefrou

semsar, semasara pl Middleman, here with rugs, can also be with real estate and rentals

senn3a A skill in making or repairing something

senna3, illa ma ghennet, katekun mestour A well-known proverb about the value of a craft: "If your craft doesn't make you rich, at least you're protected [from the cold]."

sensla A button style in Sefrou meaning "chain"

sfifa A wide band or more complex trim applied to the front and sleeves of women's robes

sha3riya "Small, short noodles," a style of jellaba button in Khenifra

shber The distance from thumb to small finger of an outstretched hand, used to measure distance in Fes embroidery and in weaving

shejarat "Trees," a stitch in both Fes and Rabat embroidery resembling trees and domes [*kbibat*]

shems A button style in Sefrou meaning "sun"

sherfat Old ladies

sherif [m], sherifa [f], shorfa [pl] Descendant of the Prophet Muhammed, much respected in Morocco

sHhada 3ala Allah The first pillar of Islam: "There is only one God and Muhammed is His Prophet." Weavers say the declaration of faith when they begin and finish a rug

shura A woman's wedding trousseau, containing embroidered table and bed linens

sidi "CD," a large flat jellaba button in Khenifra

silham A man's cape

snan l3ajel "Calf's teeth," a Middle Atlas rug design that looks like a row of small xs

snasel "Chains," the line of designs from the center to the edges of a tablecloth

souk or suq Weekly open air market, with meat (some on the hoof), vegetables, household goods, medicine, and services like dentists, barbers, tailors and others; can also mean "commercial" when describing something, such as dye

sujadat Small rugs for prayer made in the Middle Atlas

summa A kind of needle-woven button, said to be the first one, learned from Moroccan Jews; it holds up very well

sura "Picture"

taareest A kind of green clay used in place of "cooking" wool in southeastern Morocco

taabaant A cape for a little girl in southeastern Morocco; the first one is made a special way with wool donated from friends

taaban A woman's cape in southeastern Morocco; each group has its own style

taboomrekte Anti-Atlas rug design of a diamond divided into quarters, also used in old adobe buildings

tafenzad Middle Atlas rug design that looks like a line of bow ties

tafkrount "Turtle," a Middle Atlas rug motif that resembles one

tafrawt "Flying birds," a Middle Atlas rug design that resembles flying birds

taghrart Large woven saddle bag in southeastern Morocco; *tellis* in Arabic

tahaddunt, tahabant Flatweave rugs with scattered designs in pile; an old, recently revived style in the Anti-Atlas

taharoyet Traditional black wrap with colorful embroidery worn by women in southeastern Morocco

tahaykt Anti-Atlas women's cape made for a bride, in natural white wool with intricate designs on the edges, often done with natural dye in the past

talblaste Small rugs that can be knotted or flatweave or a combination in Amassine

Tamazight The dialect of Berber or Amazigh used in the Middle Atlas

tarhalt Middle Atlas flatweaves with overall designs and sequins, used to decorate the walls at weddings and for rugs at important celebrations *tarubiya* Dye made from madder root

tarz Literally "embroidery." Anti-Atlas flatweave rug style with designs that look like embroidery but are woven, OR another local name for the **teereera** design that is the same on both sides, and from the past

TashelHit or **shilHa** The dialect of Berber or Amazigh used in the Anti Atlas

taxnift or **takhnift** Anti-Atlas design found in some flatweave rugs, derived from finer wedding capes. It looks like embroidery [terz] and some women and merchants call it that, but it's definitely woven.

taxalalt Anti-Atlas design based on the fibula or brooch used to fasten women's traditional clothing

tazerbayt Large knotted rugs

tbeg, tbouka pl Palmetto grass bread basket(s)

tebban Women's capes in southeastern Morocco, also called **ahendir** or **hendira** there

tedris A needle-woven trim to edge sleeves and other edges on women's robes

teereera A traditional and old Anti-Atlas flatweave style of two-sided weaving of complex designs, the same on both sides

tehedit Black dye made from iron filings

tehendirt A woman's cape in the Middle Atlas, also called **ahaddoun**, or **hendira** in Arabic

tellis Large saddle bag in southeastern Morocco, **taghrart** in Berber

tergal A heavy French-made polyester used for early women's **jellabas**

teqshita, tqashet pl Woman's party gown in two pieces, the outer one often gauzy

tesbiH Muslim prayer beads, never made with jellaba buttons

tesmim A special layout or plan for a Middle Atlas rug

tewefee A little length added to rug warp, to account for the wool "eaten" during weaving

tidareen A design of a diamond with extensions around it [Amassine]. It means "feet" in shilHa. The same design is called **imizdareen** or "little feet" in nearby N'kob.

tighred A cash payment for washing wool in southeastern Morocco

tihuna Old style of flatweave rug with the design the same on both sides in Amassine and N'kob

tilit Middle Atlas design like a diamond, you start out with one dot, then add another in the next row, and another; it's something that grows slowly, little by little. It means something like being created.

Timahdite A breed of sheep in the Middle Atlas

timsaHa Rooster

tisuwra A white thread that attaches the threads along each end of the continuous warp to each other in southeastern Morocco

tithrite "Star," the name of the association in Ait Hamza

toudeet Oil or dirt coming from some Moroccan rugs as they are washed; probably lanolin

touta "Berry," a button style

traybiya Embroidered cloth to cover a baby carried on a woman's back

turat Heritage or traditions

twiza A traditional style of working cooperatively with others

warda A button style in Sefrou meaning "flower"

welem To go with, or complement, like colors in a rug

wida3 A design like a chain stitch in embroidery, woven along the edges of a rug or bread cloth, used to protect against the evil eye in southeastern Morocco

xatar Desire, preference

xaysh A rather loosely woven sackcloth, probably acrylic, now often used as a base for Fes embroidery on pillows

xeyyata teqlidiya A seamstress who makes traditional style clothing

xit "Thread," used for the weft yarn in many villages; ready-made yarn in the Anti-Atlas

xit harami Fake or counterfeit DMC embroidery thread

xolala, xalalat pl A brooch or fibula used in the past to fasten women's clothing at the shoulder; is used as a design in rugs

yasmina A button style in Sefrou meaning jasmine

yedd l3amila "Hand of the worker," the labor cost of an item

3ynek mizanek "Your eye is your measure"; a common proverb, used to judge wool at the market and other things

zafran "Saffron," but also used for turmeric root as a dye

zerbiya, zrabi or **zraba** Knotted or pile rugs

zizwara "Razor," an elongated hexagonal design in Fes embroidery

BIBLIOGRAPHY AND RESOURCES

Abouzeid, Leila, *Return to Childhood: The Memoir of a Modern Moroccan Woman*, Austin TX: The Center for Middle Eastern Studies, The University of Texas at Austin, 1998.

Abu-Lughod, Lila, *Do Muslim Women Need Saving?*, Cambridge MA: Harvard University Press, 2013.

Anou, http://www.theanou.com, Anou's founder has written articulately about his goals and the challenges in achieving them: https://helloanou.wordpress.com/2016/06/22/refining-the-vision-of-anou/, 2016.

Barbatti, Bruno, *Berber Carpets of Morocco. The Symbols, Origin and Meaning*, Paris: Art Creation Realisation, 2009.

Davis, Susan S., *Patience and Power: Women's Lives in a Moroccan Village*, Rochester, VT: Schenkman, 1983.

2005 Women Weavers OnLine: Rural Moroccan Women on the Internet. In *Gender and the Digital Economy: Perspectives from the Developing World.* Cecelia Ng and Swasti Mitter, Eds. Sage Publications: New Delhi, London.

DMC Library, *Morocco Embroideries,* Mulhouse France: Editions Th. De Dillmont, 1974.

Fiske, Patricia L., W. Russell Pickering, Ralph S. Yohe, *From the Far West: Carpets and Textiles of Morocco*, Washington: Textile Museum, 1980.

Grammet, Ivo and Min De Meersman, Eds., *Splendeurs du Maroc*, Tervuren, Belgium: Musee royale du l'Afrique centrale, 1998.

Hyde, Jefferson, Janice Harmer, Miriam Lorimer, W. Russell Pickering, Eds., *Windows on the Maghrib: Tribal and Urban Weavings of Morocco*, Knoxville TN: The Frank H. McClung Museum and Washington DC: The Near Eastern Art Research Center, 1992.

Ilahiane, Kheira, Moroccan television coverage of her because she was the first woman on a tribal council: https://www.youtube.com/watch?v=BN2zPc3-zHI, in French, 2016.

Mackie, Louise, *Threads of Time: Handmade Textiles for Weddings in Fez, Morocco*, Video. Toronto: Royal Ontario Museum, 1995.

Marrakeshexpress, *www.marrakeshexpress.org*, 1994-2017.

Moroccan High Commission on Population, *http://www.rgph2014.hcp.ma/*, 2014.

Messaoudi, Mohamed and Wilfied Stanzer, *First Conference on Moroccan Carpets*, Casablanca: Battaglia, 1997.

Nouh, Yasmin, *http://www.huffingtonpost.com/entry/the-beautiful-reasons-why-these-women-love-wearing-a-hijab_us_57320575e4b0bc9cb0482225*, 2016.

Paydar, Niloo Imami and Ivo Grammet, Eds., *The Fabric of Moroccan Life*, Indianapolis, IN: Indianapolis Museum of Art, 2002.

Perego, Elizabeth, (2015) *The veil or a brother's life: French manipulations of Muslim women's images during the Algerian War, 1954–62*, The Journal of North African Studies 20:3, 349-373, 2015.

Pickering, Brooke and W. Russell Pickering and Ralph S. Yohe, *Moroccan Carpets*, Washington, DC: Near Eastern Art Research Center, 1994.

Saulniers, Alfred H. and Suzanne S. Saulniers, *Ait Bou Ichaouen: Weavings of a Nomadic Berber Tribe*, Tucson AZ: Fenestra Books, 2003.

Stanzer, Wilfried, *Berber*, Graz, Austria: Helmut Reinisch, 1991.

The Artisans

Artisans eagerly welcome the opportunity to discuss their work, accept custom orders, and arrange sales. They also seek to establish contacts regarding additional opportunities, such as literacy projects and market training. The information below will facilitate such contact. You can write in English and the artisans can translate.

Contact the following Timnay Association artisans through the Anou website: Aicha Seqqat, Ijja Seqqat, Anaya Seqqat, Jamila Samaa, Kebira Aglaou, Fatima El Mennouny, Fatima Id Rahou, and Rqia Ait Taleb: http://www.theanou.com/store/84-taznakht-association-timnay-morocco

Cooperative Assabirate: cooperativeassabirate2000@gmail.com

Habiba Lrhachi, Fatima Fdil, and Fatima Lrhachi: mimihabiba@hotmail.com

Amina Yabis and Aziza Bourouaha: amina_yabis@yahoo.fr

Rachida Ousbigh through the Anou website: http://www.theanou.com/store/6-khenifra-womens-cooperative-khenifra-morocco and also in the U.S.: https://ifamonline.org/collections/khenifra

Samira Benayad: benayyadsamira@yahoo.fr

Fadma Wadal, through her grandson: mohamed_flilou@yahoo.com or through his museum site at http://www.musee-tilila.com/

Kheira Ilahiane and Fatima Mama Ilahiane: kheira_ilahiane@yahoo.fr_ or contact her at the family's oasis B&B: www.maisondhotessahara.com

Kenza Oulaghda through Anou website: http://www.theanou.com/store/13-association-tithrite-ait-hamza-morocco or kenzatithrite1@gmail.com

Contact the following artisans through Susan S. Davis: Fadma Buhassi, Aicha Duha, Zinebe Bounouara, Fatima Benayad, Aicha Al Borbouch, and Fdila Azreg: sdavis@uslink.net

Cultural Tours

Susan Schaefer Davis leads cultural tours to Morocco, offering in depth contact with several Moroccans, some featured in this book. One tour is general and another more focused on textiles, many of which travelers will learn about and may try. Contact Susan at sdavis@uslink.net for more information.

Photography Credits

Susan Schaefer Davis provided the photographs on the following pages:

44, 47 at right, 93, 94 at right, 96–106, 150–151.

INDEX